www.wadehaggard.com

I'm in Dutch!

A Laugh-Out-Loud Guide to Dutch-Oven Cooking

Wade P. Haggard

Wade P. Haggard

Copyright © 2014 by Wade P. Haggard. All rights reserved.

ISBN-13:
978-1507808788

ISBN-10:
150780878X

Library of Congress Control Number: 2015904055

CreateSpace Independent Publishing Platform, North Charleston, SC

DEDICATION

To my friends and family, I owe a debt of thanks. Those who are continually forced to listen to my ramblings yet still remain by my side are the truest examples of fierce loyalty and friendship.

CONTENTS

Acknowledgments i
1 Introduction 1
2 A Brief History of the Dutch Oven 5
3 What You Need to Know and Have 9
4 Beef 27
5 Chicken 47
6 Pork 63
7 Bread 79
8 Breakfast 97
9 Chili and Casseroles 111
10 Fish and Game 127
11 Sides 137
12 Desserts 151
13 Sauces and Rubz 174
Index 186
About the Author 188

I'm in Dutch!

ACKNOWLEDGMENTS

Thank you, Mother, for allowing me to turn your kitchen
into a science lab in my younger years.

Thank you, boys, for your willingness
to live in an endless taste-testing session.

Thank you to my wife for humoring and supporting my crazy ideas.

Wade P. Haggard

1 Introduction

I am and have always been a "food person." I love a good meal. What could be better than sharing a meal with those closest to you? Friends and family united around the dinner table or a picnic table talking and sharing stories, feelings, triumph, and defeat. I have learned a lot listening to my children as we conversed while preparing our dinner. Think of the deep and meaningful conversations you've had while tailgating and eating from a foam plate in freezing temperatures with friends and competitors, cheering and jeering in rivalry and camaraderie. For an inside view of one's culture, we only need to look as far as what is eaten, where, when, and how.

I have to admit—one of my great frustrations in life is looking up a recipe, only to find that it starts out with a "box of" or "package of." I harbor no ill will toward shortcuts in cooking, but I like to see how stuff works! I have no problem using a packaged cake mix for a cobbler; it is easy and, given the situation, may be called for. However, I want to know how it came together. One goal I have for this book is to provide you with the power of either solution. Most of the recipes will be "from scratch," and I mention shortcuts, where applicable. The roots of some recipes are based on a package, and I will point out those instances as well. To the cook goes the power.

The structure and flow of this book is a bit different from the typical recipe book. I like to include easy solutions and shortcuts, plus a few silly stories. If one technique and recipe works for multiple types or cuts of meat, I will mention it. Campfire stories are a time-honored tradition, so you will get some tall tales, but the recipes and instruction are legit. Recipes in this book may be a touch spicy for some, so adjust as you see fit, and do not be afraid to play with the seasonings. Dutch-oven cooking is as much art as science, and both need to be present for great-tasting food.

My family loves the outdoors. Over the years, as I have volunteered with the Boy Scouts of America, as well as in my community and church, I have done Dutch-oven cooking for groups from 2 to 150 individuals. I have had some great successes, as well as some bitter and burnt tasting defeats. I have experienced the euphoria of the elements and actions working together to create the perfect relaxed and happy setting with a great dinner. I have also experienced the world stacked against me, the wind and rain attacking every coal to humble my cooking pride.

Oddly enough, the amount of food being prepped and the number of people being fed altar the equation only a small bit. Dutch-oven cooking is perfect for feeding the masses, and the recipes included here are big. Don't be afraid to split them for smaller numbers. I would hope, as you begin your experience, I have prepared you and empowered you with the knowledge and tools you need for a positive Dutch-oven cooking experience.

Ultimately, you will decide what the purpose of this book is and how to use it. You may want a few ideas to add variety to your established Dutch-oven knowledge, or you may be at point "0" and want to walk through the entire process. The information, methods, and recipes in this book should provide you either opportunity. If you want my two cents' worth, which is like a two-cent discount on this book, I would read it cover to cover and visualize the process and the recipes. Yes, I know it is a cookbook with recipes, but it is interesting enough that I believe you will enjoy it. The visualization will give you experience, and the first time you cook Dutch, you will feel much more like you have done it before. As you read, you will also gain ideas for condiments and sides that may appeal to you and your family or group. Please refrain from licking the pages; a scratch-and-lick version may be available at a later date. Look for items in season, find the best cuts of meat, and enjoy each bite!

We do not know what we do not know.

We have not been where we dare not go.

We cannot see where we will not look.

Dread of the wet stems crossing the brook.

I, like many, chose to bide my time.

But time won't bide; it passes us by.

A voice of potential roused my ear.

Turns out "not trying," was all to fear.

—Wade P. Haggard

2 A Brief History of the Dutch Oven

There are many types of Dutch ovens, ranging from ceramic and clay to cast iron covered in enamel. Outside the United States and in many other English-speaking countries, Dutch ovens are sometimes called "casserole dishes." The Japanese refer to them as "Tetsunabe" or "Sac." All over the world, variations of the oven can be found. It is good to know the various names of Dutch ovens. When you see a recipe calling for cooking in an oven at 350°F in a casserole dish, you will recognize the ability to cook the same recipe in your Dutch oven. However, for the purpose of this book, we will be using a black cast iron, thick-walled cooking pot with a wire bail handle and a tight fitting, slightly concave, rimmed lid, made specifically for hot-charcoal cooking. This configuration is known as a camping, cowboy, or chuckwagon Dutch oven.

Did you know that the first Dutch oven appeared early in the eleventh century? A Viking iron crafter by the name of Knotu Boianceson cast a small, circular iron watercraft to attack villages up and down the coast. His experiment went horribly wrong, and he and his apprentice, Soonk Ancorstyne, disappeared on their maiden voyage. The technology was lost until the seventeenth century, when it is said that a mermaid, doing some spring-cleaning, removed the watercraft from her reef and placed it on the beach near a small village in Holland.

The village outcast and maker of trouble, named for the Norse Lord of Mischief and Mayhem, Loki, found the watercraft. Loki was the illegitimate son of the village ironworker. He multiplied the vessel in small form, measuring about 12" round for prototype purposes, and began pitching his idea for the watercraft. The fine sands used for mold making and excellent artisanship of the Dutch allowed for casting a smooth surface with a beautiful sheen. Although the idea for the boat did not develop, many used the prototypes for cooking, and Loki's "oven" soon caught on. Loki became a rich man. True story—well, that's what I heard.

People in the newly colonized America loved the Dutch oven for its versatility and durability. It was the one pot to use for all cooking. Stewing, frying, baking, roasting, and boiling could be accomplished in a single pot. An entire meal could be prepared and left to cook while other chores were attended to. The Dutch oven became so valuable that George Washington's mother left mention of her kitchen "ironware" in her will. She may have been referring to her kitchen "underwear"; she had terrible handwriting and was well known for cooking in her long johns. Either way, the recipient was instructed to "clean the bottoms regularly," good advice for both situations.

Dutch ovens traveled along with the pioneers who were opening the West and exploring a new wilderness. The Mormon handcart companies proudly displayed their Dutch ovens on the front of their carts. The Dutch oven is the official state cooking pot of Utah, Arkansas, and Texas. Many other states are petitioning at this time for an officially recognized cooking pot.

As with all things introduced to the Americas, changes and innovation evolved the Dutch oven. Legs on the bottom to keep the pot above the coals were added, maybe out of necessity of the traveler who had an open campfire for cooking. (Direct contact with coals can smother them.) Pioneers used buffalo chips for fire fuel as they crossed the plains. A phrase soon emerged to describe food cooked with such fuel and has endured in the American language to this day. As a result, a lip was added around the pot's lid to keep coals out of the food when the lid was removed.

Dutch ovens are especially suited for slow cooking over long periods. Anything you can cook in a typical home oven can be adapted to the Dutch oven, and vice versa. Breads, cakes, pies, and biscuits can be cooked easily in the Dutch. Dutch ovens are also great for stacking one on top of the other and using the coals atop one to heat the bottom of the next. It is not uncommon for me to cook three Dutch ovens high at a single event. That way, the main dish, sides, and dessert are ready at the same time.

3 What You Need to Know and Have

I once met a man with gum in his hands and a head smothered in PB&J.

Quirking one brow as if to ask "how," his face responded "Follow me this way."

I thought as we walked that maybe we'd talk, but the silence rang loudly all mile.

Glimpsing his blouse was official Boy Scout, I assumed he'd explain in a while.

We walked into camp littered with scamps of an age from twelve to thirteen.

The ruckus and mayhem began to betray them, and my lungs filled with air for a scream.

But the gentle Scoutmaster was quite a bit faster and introduced me as a man to be saved.

"I went and nabbed him, so you come and grab him, and resume attempting first aid!"

—Wade P. Haggard

The Checklist

- Dutch oven: Check

- Pizza pan to set coals on: Check

- Bag of charcoal: Check

- Tongs to use in moving coals around: Check

- Leather gloves: Check

- Charcoal chimney: Check

- Lighter fluid: Check

- Long-handled lighter: Check

- Newspaper: Check

- Lid-lifting tool (Long-handled channel lock pliers work great.): Check

- Roll of paper towels: Check

- Vegetable oil: Check

(In the sections that follow, I explain each of the items mentioned above and abstain from saying "Check.")

The Dutch Oven

So you want a Dutch oven? Where do you get such a thing? Well, the answers are endless and depend on your needs. If you are going to buy new, just about any camping store, surplus store, or farm store will have a good selection. As mentioned in the previous chapter, for the purpose of this book we use only cast iron, not aluminum. If you want a cheaper used Dutch, try yard sales and thrift stores. A little surface rust and dirt should not scare you; it can be easily cleaned. If you buy used, you will need to clean and season your Dutch (see the next section). If you purchased a new Dutch, chances are it came preseasoned; just be sure to read the box and instructions. I prefer the 14"version, although 12" is pretty standard as well. Throughout this book, I use the 14" round, 5" deep Dutch oven, which will set you back about $60-$90. How smooth the inside of the Dutch oven is determines its worth. Smoother is better, just like shaving and pancake batter. Remember the Dutch and their fine sand?

Seasoning Your Dutch

I'm sure you have heard the term "season" before, but what does it mean? Well, in short, you are going to burn oil into the porous surface of your oven. Remember, smoother is better. It sounds bizarre, but in truth it is very similar to the Teflon process and has similar results. We season to protect and create a nonstick surface. I am making a couple of assumptions: first, that this is the first time you have seasoned your Dutch, and second, that you will never allow soap to touch your Dutch. Yes, you read correctly; soap is the enemy. From this point forward, we will use hot water, heat, and oil to clean the Dutch.

OK, I can hear the yelling as you read, so let me explain the soap issues, myths, and truths. Remember the Dutch and their fine sand? The fine, dry sand was used for making molds in which to cast the iron, leaving a very smooth and thus less porous surface. Soap, like everything else, gets into your Dutch's pores. If you have a high-quality, usually older, very smooth Dutch, this probably isn't a problem. If you own a "rougher"-bottom Dutch, the soap can linger and end up in your food. Soap is difficult to remove from the Dutch. High heat and oil, on the other hand, are what you want in your Dutch. If you decide you absolutely have to use soap, go right ahead. Just rinse the oven thoroughly with hot water and reseason it when you are done. Also, plan a bubble blowing activity for your next cookout.

You may not want to undertake the seasoning process in the house. Go outside and use your BBQ grill, or if you can, use your neighbor's oven. Cook them a cobbler; all will be forgiven. Cobblers are a lot like Jedi mind wipes. OK, if you insist, you can use your conventional oven; it may get stinky in your house if you do not have excellent ventilation. If your home oven has a self-cleaning option, you are in luck. The self-cleaning option is the best and easiest way to season your Dutch.

The Seasoning Party

Step 1: Clean your Dutch. Use hot water and a scouring pad, or the self-cleaning oven cycle works great.

Step 2: Prepare your cooking area. Use a pizza pan that is slightly larger than the Dutch. (You should have this for later use as well, think "dollar store.")

Step 3: Cover the Dutch in vegetable oil. Cover every surface thoroughly, inside and out, including the lid. Use a paper towel and coat the Dutch; it should not drip oil in the oven.

Step 4: With the pizza pan on the bottom rack in the oven or on the grill, place the Dutch upside down on the pan. I like to use a metal spoon to create space between the Dutch and the pan. Place the lid on top so it is resting on the Dutch's legs.

Step 5: Cook the empty Dutch at 475°F for 1 hour (or use the self-clean cycle), shut off the oven or grill, and allow the Dutch to sit for another hour. Keep an eye on the process; watch for heavy smoke, and have a fire extinguisher on hand.

Step 6: When the Dutch is cool enough to handle, remove it and wipe it clean with a paper towel.

Step 7: Repeat steps three through six until a beautiful, even sheen is achieved (twice should work).

Step 8: Fiercely defend your Dutch from any wannabe do-gooder wielding soap!

This one time at Dutch-oven camp, I used our best cookie sheets and silverware on a Dutch-oven project. Needless to say, they turned several shades of black. A good rule of thumb when approaching Dutch-oven cooking is not to use any item you are not willing to turn black and/or burn. Hot mitts, gloves, pans, spoons, tongs, spatulas, forks, etc.—all will turn black and/or burn. This is why you will want a dedicated Dutch oven kit. (Again, think "dollar store.")

Charcoal Preparation

There are many ways to ignite charcoal. It can be a bit thorny if the wind is howling and can get a bit dangerous if you are on your patio. Check local laws and ordinances to avoid any unpleasant visits from law enforcement or angry neighbors. With any luck, the delicious aromas of your food will be the attractant. A couple of must-have items: leather gloves, long tongs for grabbing coals (cheapies are fine), a pizza pan, and, in my opinion, a charcoal chimney. The pizza pan is a must-have to place coals on and keep them dry and off the wet ground. Also, it will keep your Dutch from sinking into sand or dirt and smothering your coals. The chimney also makes a great lid stand.

One choice for lighting coals is the common approach of stacking the coals into a pyramid and using lighter fluid. Stack coals in a pyramid in your fire ring, on a grill, or on a pizza pan on the ground. Spray liberally with lighter fluid (use your noggin here, folks) and use a long match or long-handled lighter to ignite the coals safely.

Do not spray lighter fluid on the smoldering briquettes—bad idea. The lighter fluid's stream could easily ignite the squirting fluid and the bottle, resulting in severe damage. If your coals need a boost, give more air to already burning coals. Speed up ignition by gently fanning the briquettes until you see flames in several spots. A dust pan works

great as a fan. Let them burn for a time, and then repeat the fanning process if needed, a few times. There will be an obvious point when the briquettes are happy; they will ultimately form a nice, gray ash—usually about ten minutes, but it varies by brand.

I like the charcoal chimney; it is my preferred method. It is easy and involves roughly the same process as above, but it is self-contained. A rolled-up piece of newspaper formed into a ring at the bottom of the chimney works great if you wish to avoid using a large amount of lighter fluid. I use a small, single, 30,000 BTU burner below my chimney to start my coals; it is fast and helps when I am cooking multiple ovens for large groups of people. For the purposes of this book, we will assume that you do not have the burner.

Regulating and Determining Temperature

A host of variables can affect temperature in the oven, including ambient temperature, humidity, wind, sunlight, and elevation. Charcoal selection is important as well; I like to use the same brand of charcoal all the time, to achieve consistent results. How the coals are placed on the oven changes the heat factor and form of cooking. A good rule of thumb for 325°F to 350°F is Dutch oven size minus three coals on bottom, and plus three coals on top. For this reason, with a 14" Dutch oven, (14 – 3 = 11), 11 coals on bottom, (14 + 3 = 17) 17 coals on top should get me 325°F to 350°F. For every two coals added (top and bottom), I get an additional 25° increase in temperature. So, for a 14" Dutch oven, 13 coals on bottom and 19 on top will give me about 350°F to 375°F. In most recipes, I use 12–14 coals on bottom and 16–18 on top. I usually err on the high side, 14 bottom and 18 top. You will need to gain experience with your

Dutch oven, environment, and type of charcoal to find your preferred proportion.

Now let's talk about the "ring" method. Because coals vary in size, and you may on occasion use lump charcoal, the ring method helps out where math fails. Simply make a ring of coals, before you light them, around the top edge of the lid and the bottom edge of the oven. The coals around the circumference of the top and bottom will closely add up to the math method and will give you the medium cooking temperature you are looking for, 325°F to 350°F. Once lit, place the coals evenly in a checkerboard pattern.

Another method of determining the temperature is the hand-hold method. With the lid off your heated oven, place your flat palm in the center vertically and horizontally (not touching). Start counting in seconds. When the heat is uncomfortable, move your hand. For each second you hold your hand there, subtract 50 degrees from 600. For example:

1 second = 550°F

2 seconds = 500°F

3 seconds = 450°F

And so on.... Now, this is not a super accurate way to determine the temperature because we all have different tolerances and interpretations of uncomfortable, but it helps.

In a picnic setting, your coals will last about 45 minutes. You will need to start prepping more coals at the 35-minute mark to continue with longer cooking sessions.

A Great Exercise with Your New Dutch Oven

After you read through this chapter and are comfortable preparing coals to cook, prepare a batch of 32 coals. Place 14 coals on your pizza pan in an even, circular, checkerboard pattern, beginning on the outside and moving to the center. Place your Dutch on the coals, and place an oven thermometer in the center. Place the lid on the Dutch and the remaining 18 coals in a similar circular checkerboard pattern. Let the Dutch cook for 15–20 minutes, then remove the lid. The temperature on the thermometer is a good indicator; it should be about 350°F. Now you have a good starting point. Adjust by one or two coals, based on your findings.

Adjusting Charcoal Placement for Type of Cooking

Here are some guidelines based on how you plan to use your Dutch:

- To bake in your Dutch, move one-third of your bottom coals to the lid.

- Roasting requires an even number on top and bottom.

- For stewing and simmering, use two-thirds bottom heat to one-third top heat.

- For boiling and frying, put all of the coals on the bottom. Use rocks or bricks to lift the Dutch and create space. Coals need air to burn. (If you plan to boil and deep-fry frequently, invest in a propane burner, a big one, 30,000 BTU.)

"But Wade…that's not really Dutch-oven cooking," I can hear huffed in a nasally, whiny voice.

Well, yes it is. The pioneers used whatever fuel they had, as did the Dutch and other Europeans before them. Why shouldn't you? This book and the recipes within contain the information you need to fry and boil on charcoal, and it works. But if my happiness were at stake, I'd spend the $30 or so to get a simple, single, 30K BTU burner. Bigger works too.

Optional But Happy Equipment

- Infrared thermometer

    I really like having a temperature gauge on my Dutch; it helps a lot in the winter months. You can pick one up at your local "cheap tool" store for about $30, and it makes an awesome gift for any Dutcher.

- 30K BTU burner

    I use my burner to light coals in my chimney; it takes three minutes to get a batch going. Frying and boiling are made simple as well.

Changing Coals

During your cooking sessions, you will have to swap coals as they die for fresh, new, hot coals. As coals fade, your temp varies, and depending on the time of year, this equation will change greatly. Wintertime will find you swapping coals at the 30-minute mark if it is utterly rigid cold outside. Summer days in the heat are more forgiving, and your coals may burn strong for 50 minutes without a problem.

One technique I have used and find helpful, especially in long cooking sessions, is the "minion method." With this method, we are going to place a batch of unlit coals in a pattern on our lid and pizza pan, sometimes two batches. Then, when we are ready to begin cooking, we will place our torched coals, one by one, alongside and touching our unlit coals. Over the course of the next 30 minutes, our active coals will heat up and light our unlit coals, and our heat will move gradually along the path of the charcoal.

This method does not work well for heat-sensitive foods like cakes and breads that need the lid and bottom rotated. Dishes such as stew, chili, slow-cooked fatty pork, and beef roasts are prime for this method. Set it up and go about your day, checking back only occasionally. Practice once or twice before relying on it for a successful meal.

Using What You Have

I hope you are like me and Dutch year 'round. Dutch at home, while tailgating, at your community center or church, while camping, for friends and family, and on occasion, just to see "what would happen if...." The various environments present challenges and benefits. At home, on my patio, I can use my full kitchen, fridge, freezer, stove, microwave, and so on. In the field, I have my Dutch oven and a spoon. Your approach will have to change based on your circumstance.

Part of the fun is using what you have. For example, when you are camping and you want to make pancakes and bacon for breakfast, you will use the Dutch oven and the lid separately, each as a cooking surface. After you cook the bacon, use the grease as the fat for cooking your pancakes, hash browns, and eggs. If this bothers you, clean out your Dutch and use butter or oil. I love bacon-flavored anything and everything.

The Wind

As I mentioned earlier, Dutch-oven cooking is as much an art as a science. You will have to develop an intuitive process for dealing with the elements. Wind is by far my most antagonistic nemesis. Wind changes heat, temperature, placement, cooking times, and charcoal-burning time, and it generally will seek to mess up everything about your experience. You can find domes and other devices for sale on the Internet to protect your oven from the elements while cooking, but these items are not cheap. Get creative and work with what you have. The best tool you have is your noggin, so be resourceful and look for solutions. I usually have a chair or folding table with me; lying on its side, it can provide two sides of wind protection. If I use the table and nestle in against my truck, I can surround the Dutch oven with a windscreen. Several times, I have mentioned a trip to the dollar store. If I lived in an area where wind was a constant burden to my Dutch-oven experience, I would purchase three or four cookie sheets and a roll of wire from the dollar store. I would place them in a triangular fashion on their sides around my oven with one on top and create a $5 dome of my own. Because I do not live in such an area, I make do with what I have on hand.

Lid Cooking

Your Dutch's lid is an added cook surface and can be a great help. There are a couple things it is important to know before you plan a full-on lid-cooking assault. The lid loses heat much faster than the entire Dutch. Thus, it takes more briquettes to keep the lid hot. Throughout this book, I list a number of briquettes for 14" lid cooking, typically 22–24. It is important to remember that you want a blanket of coals under the lid, providing complete coverage for cooking. Use rocks or bricks to lift the Dutch and create space. Again, coals need air to burn. If I had a choice, I would use my trusted propane burner for lid cooking. If you do not have a propane burner, put it on your birthday wish list. Warming tortillas and such won't need quite the firepower.

A Thought on Flavor

Taste your food as you cook. All too often, people ask me, "What went wrong?" As I taste the dish, it is missing salt, pepper, or herbs—in short, flavor. Limes are a great way to enhance the flavor of many foods; you will notice that I use a lot of lime juice. Fresh lime juice only, never concentrate. Worcestershire and bouillon are the magic duo for beef; they will make your burgers better than any you have ever had, and you will notice that I use the combination frequently. *You can't over herb!* Well, OK, you probably can. I am far more afraid of under flavoring than over flavoring. Be careful with salt, but taste as you cook, and add herbs, spices, or sauces.

A Thought on Bacon

Yes, please. You can't have too much bacon. No, really. If you set out to make a cheeseburger, and at the end of the cooking session all you have is several pounds of perfectly cooked bacon, would it be a bad thing?

The Example

Let's walk through a simple recipe from start to finish as an example. One of the easiest and most tasty Dutch-oven treats is BBQ chicken. Read this section and visualize yourself doing each step of the process. Visualize your surroundings and what you will have to work with.

First, gather your Dutch-oven implements: Dutch oven, lid tool or channel-lock pliers, bag of charcoal, chimney, long-handled lighter, newspaper, lighter fluid, pizza pan, gloves, paper towels, veggie oil, and tongs. Place your items on a table, tailgate, or tarp on the ground, depending on your location.

For now, you will use packaged ingredients; later you will learn to do it all from scratch. The following recipe is the stripped-down, easy version. Later in the book, recipes get a bit tastier and more complicated.

BBQ Chicken

- 8 chicken quarters, leg and thigh preferred, bone in, skin on (Make sure your chicken is completely thawed and drained, or you will have soupy BBQ.)
- 2 c. of your favorite BBQ sauce
- 1 medium onion
- 1 stick of butter, 8 tbsp.
- 2 tsp. salt
- 2 tsp. pepper

Simple, huh? You are also going to need some items to prepare the meal: a knife, a cutting board, measuring cups, measuring spoons, and some cleaning supplies. Again, the dollar store can be your friend. If you cook on the go a lot, having a tote with all your stuff in one place can be a great help.

Let's get cooking. Start by finding a clear area to place you pizza pan; this is your cooking area. Get out of the wind and on a stable surface (the ground). What is beneath will get very hot, so if you do not want dead grass, choose wisely. My brick patio works great; concrete also works great. The pizza tin will keep the mess off the ground and should keep the surface from discoloring, but again, use your noggin.

Now get your briquettes going. Roll a sheet of newspaper into a doughnut shape the same circumference as your briquette chimney. Place the paper doughnut in the bottom of the chimney. Add 15 briquettes on top of the paper and spray liberally with lighter fluid. Think 1 Mississippi, 2 Mississippi, then add 15 more coals and repeat the lighter-fluid process. Place your charcoal-filled, lighter-fluid-soaked chimney on your pizza pan, and light it at arm's length with your long-handled lighter. *Whoosh!* You made fire—congratulations!

The briquettes need to get happy for about 10 to 15 minutes. While they are getting up to speed, you are going to prepare your chicken. Start by separating the leg from the thigh on each piece. Slice into the joint, and it will separate easily. You can also buy all legs or all thighs; the process works the same for all. After each piece is separated, pour a tablespoon or so of oil in the bottom of your Dutch oven and spread it around. Slice your onion into five or six rings and separate them. Place them all around the bottom of the Dutch. Season your chicken with salt and pepper, and place the chicken on top of the onion slices. Cut the butter into several chunks and place them on top of the chicken, evenly around the Dutch. Now pour BBQ sauce evenly over all ingredients in the Dutch. Place the lid on top.

When the briquettes have turned at least 30 percent gray, start placing them evenly in a circular pattern on the pizza pan, from the outside to the center. Use 12–14 on the bottom. Set your Dutch on top of the pattern of briquettes and center it with them. On the lid, place the remaining 16 to 18 briquettes in a similar pattern. Congrats—you are cooking!

Every 15 to 20 minutes, turn the lid and the Dutch one-quarter of a turn in opposite directions. This movement allows the contents of the Dutch to cook evenly over the coals and avoids a long-term hot spot. Do not lift the lid off the food and release the inner heat; it will twist in place sliding on the Dutch.

The chicken needs to cook for 1 hour and 15–30 minutes. At the 30-minute mark, repeat the charcoal process to have fresh coals ready at the 45-minute mark because the briquettes usually last about 45 minutes. Remove the Dutch and place the new coals alongside the old, place the Dutch oven back on top of the coals, and place fresh coals on top in a similar fashion. The 45-minute mark is also a good time to peek at the chicken and see how it is doing. Move it around, if necessary, to avoid overcooking in some areas. Remember, your chimney makes a great lid stand.

A Final Thought

You are ready to go! Dutch-oven cooking should be fun and adventurous; do not be afraid to experiment. Cook a few items that are in your realm of experience, and then branch out into something you never thought of doing. Most importantly, share your experiences with family and friends.

4 Beef

Why Dairy Farmers Make Good Scoutmasters

- Cows can detect odors up to six miles away; Scouts can create odors up to six miles away.

- Both cows and Scouts have favorite friends and become stressed when separated.

- Cows have about 300 degrees of vision, with blind spots only directly in front of and behind them. Scouts similarly have blinds spots in front of them, especially when something needs to be picked up or cleaned.

- Cows and Scouts account for about 20 percent of greenhouse gas emissions.

- Cows and Scouts each consume about 100 lbs. of feed per day; both prefer grazing.

- Cattle produce about 500 L of methane gas a day; Scouts do this as well.

- Both Scouts and cows chew in large, circular motions with their mouths open.

- Cows sleep about four hours a day. Scouts can sleep up to four hours a day but prefer to save up sleep time for the drive home and use it all at once.

- Both cattle and Scouts share approximately 80 percent of their genes with humans.

Introduction to Beef

For many beef dishes, the preparation process is the same. By adjusting seasoning, serving style, and side dishes, you can create a new meal with little effort. For example, the beef round steak, which you can usually find on sale and is a relatively inexpensive cut of beef, is excellent for creating a "steak tip" meal. These meals are also excellent for introducing youth to cooking Dutch.

Another good choice that is sometimes on sale is sirloin. Sirloin is a bit more flexible with cooking variation, and it reacts well to grilling and stewing. Either cut will work for the following recipes. I select sirloin when possible.

Remember your coal preparation!

Steak Tips

- 3–4 lbs. round steak, cubed to 2" x 2" (give or take 25 percent)
- 1 medium onion, diced fine
- 1 clove garlic, crushed and diced
- 1 tsp. black pepper
- 1 tsp. salt
- 1 cube beef bouillon, crushed fine*
- 1 tsp. onion powder*
- 2 tbsp. Worcestershire*
- 2 tbsp. vegetable oil

A combination of Worcestershire, onion, and bouillon is sometimes called "Beef Magic."

- Place a 14" Dutch oven on top of 22–24 coals, spread evenly. Add 2 tbsp. of vegetable oil.
- Add cubed steak; spread evenly to begin browning.
- Add salt, bouillon, Worcestershire, and onion.
- Brown for 5 minutes.
- Add pepper, onion powder, and garlic.
- Stir and cook a 2 minutes to allow the ingredients to blend around the steak.

It is time to make a couple of decisions now. What will your sides be? Where do you want your flavor profile to go? If you want to, you can continue cooking for 20 minutes or until your desired doneness is reached. I recommend that you read on. The following pages contain some "saucy" ideas.

Steak Tips Teriyaki Style

- o 1 batch steak tips (p. 30)
- o 2 c. Tenacious Teriyaki Sauce (p. 179) (Or you can substitute 2 c. of your favorite Teriyaki sauce.)

- Add the sauce to browned steak tips; stir to mix.
- Place lid on oven with 14–16 coals on top, 12–14 coals on bottom.
- Cook for 30 minutes.
- Rotate lid and pot one-quarter turn every 15–20 minutes without removing the lid.
- When the steak is done, thicken the sauce by removing the lid and placing all coals beneath the Dutch. (Turn your lid upside down and rest the steak there until the sauce is thick, about 10 minutes.)
- Add the steak back into the sauce, then remove the Dutch from the heat.
- Serve over white or brown rice, with fried rice (p. 147), or with a baked potato.
- For a great beef and broccoli dish, add chopped broccoli the last 15 minutes of cooking time.

If you leave the steak in the sauce as you try to reduce, the steak will become dry and overcooked.

Steak Tips BBQ Sweet/Hot Style

- 1 batch steak tips (p. 30)
- 2 c. Best BBQ Sauce Ever! (p. 177)
- 2 tbsp. The Rub (p. 181)

- Add sauce and 1 stick butter to browned steak tips; stir to mix.
    - Substitute 2T olive oil for the stick of butter if you wish, or omit.
- Place lid on oven with 14–16 coals on top, 12–14 coals on the bottom.
- Cook for 30 minutes.
- Rotate lid and pot one-quarter turn every 15–20 minutes without removing the lid.
- When steak is done, thicken the sauce by removing the lid and placing all coals beneath the Dutch. (Turn your lid upside down and rest the steak there until the sauce is thick, about 10 minutes.)
- Add the steak back into sauce; remove the Dutch from the heat.
- Serve on a roll, over white or brown rice, or on top of a baked potato.

Steak Tips BBQ Vinegar Style

- o 1 batch steak tips (p. 30)
- o 1 c. BBQ Vinegar-Style Sauce (p. 178)

- Place lid on oven with 14–16 coals on top, 12–14 coals on bottom.
- Cook for 30 minutes.
- Rotate lid and pot one-quarter turn every 15–20 minutes without removing the lid.
- When steak is done, thicken the sauce by removing the lid and placing all coals beneath the Dutch. (Turn your lid upside down and rest the steak there until the sauce is thick, about 10 minutes.)
- Add the sauce and one stick of butter to browned steak tips; stir to mix. Omit butter if desired.
- Serve on a roll.
- This mix is excellent served with hash browns!

Steak Tips Rosemary and Garlic Style

- 1 batch steak tips (p. 30)
- 3–4 sprigs of fresh rosemary, with just the leaves chopped
    - Substitute 2T dried rosemary if desired.
- 2 cloves of garlic, minced
- 1 c. water
- 2 tbsp. flour

- Mix flour and water into a slurry.
- Add slurry, rosemary, garlic, and one stick of butter to browned Steak Tips; stir to mix.
- Place lid on oven with 16–18 coals on top and 12–14 coals on the bottom.
- Cook for 40 minutes.
- Rotate lid and pot one-quarter turn every 15–20 minutes without removing the lid.
- Serve on top of Italian Potatoes (p. 140) or with mashed potatoes.

Did you know you could use an inexpensive coffee grinder to grind your spices and herbs? You can purchase a coffee grinder at most "Super-Mart" stores.

Steak and Potatoes in One Pot

- 1 batch steak tips (p. 30)
- 6–8 potatoes (medium to large to get a good 1:1 steak-to-potato mix), cubed
- 2 tbsp. olive oil
- 3 tbsp. Italian Rub (p. 182)

    (You can substitute one package of dry Italian dressing mix for the Italian Rub.)

- Coat cubed potatoes with 2 tbsp. olive oil.
- Sprinkle seasoning mix over oil-coated potatoes.
- Add potatoes to browned Steak Tips and stir.
- Place lid on oven with 14–16 coals on top, 12–14 coals on bottom.
- Cook for 1 hour and 15 minutes.
- Rotate lid and pot one-quarter turn every 15–20 minutes without removing the lid.
- Add fewer potatoes and add some carrots for a little variety. This recipe works great with yellow sweet potatoes, too.

Swiss Steak

- 3 lbs. round steak or sirloin, cut and pounded into palm-sized ¼" thin steaks (Pounding the steak flat will help tenderize it. You can also use a needle device.)
- ¾ c. flour
- ¼ lb. bacon
- 1 large onion, thinly sliced
- 2 cloves garlic, minced
- 2 stalks celery, chopped
- 1 tbsp. tomato paste
- 1 14.5-oz. can diced tomatoes
- 1 tsp. smoked paprika
- 1 tbsp. Worcestershire
- 2 c. beef broth

- Season each side of the steaks with a dash of salt, pepper, and onion powder.
- Dredge each side with flour.
- Place a 14" Dutch oven on top of 22–24 coals, evenly spread.
- Render bacon of fat and remove the bacon chunks. The oil should shimmer; be careful not to get it too hot, about 350°F.
- Brown each side of each steak approximately two minutes, then remove from the oven and set each aside as it is done. (The clean side of the Dutch-oven lid works great for collecting the steaks.)
- In the drippings and oil of the Dutch oven, add the onion, garlic, and celery and sauté for 2 minutes.
- Add the tomato paste and combine.
- Add the tomatoes, paprika, oregano, Worcestershire, and broth; stir to combine.

- Return the steaks to the pot, submerging them in the liquid.

- Replace the bottom coals with new coals (12–14). (They have been cooking long enough that they will now begin to lose their heat.)

- Place lid on oven with 16–18 coals on top, 12–14 coals on the bottom.

- Cook for 45 minutes.

- Rotate lid and pot one-quarter turn every 15–20 minutes without removing the lid.

- Serve with green beans.

Did you know that you can fan your coals with a dustpan to give them an extra boost if they aren't catching fire quickly enough? You can use a cheap pizza pan to protect your patio from discoloring while lighting coals and cooking.

Carne Asada Tacos

- 3 lbs. round steak or sirloin, cut and pounded into palm-sized ¼" thin steaks
- 2 tbsp. oil (vegetable or peanut)
- 2 dozen corn tortillas
- 2 limes, zested and juiced
- 2 limes, cut into small wedges
- 2 tsp. salt
- 1 tsp. black pepper
- ¼ head of cabbage, sliced thin
- 2 cucumbers, sliced into rounds

- Place Dutch oven on 20–22 coals; add oil.
- Season each steak with salt, pepper, lime zest, and lime juice (best if marinated overnight).
- Place Dutch lid upside down on 14–16 coals, like a skillet.
- Cook steaks in Dutch oven for 5–6 minutes on each side or until desired doneness is achieved.
- Warm tortillas on Dutch-oven lid.
- Slice steak into small strips or chop into chunks.
- Serve on warm tortillas with salsa, chopped cabbage, a wedge of lime, and sliced cucumbers.

Beef Brisket

Beef brisket can be tough if not cooked low-'n-slow. Many recipes call for a tenderizer; I personally do not care for that approach. Most enzymes used for tenderizing do not deactivate until a temperature of 160°F. I like my meat rare to medium rare, which means any leftover meat will turn to mush as the enzymes continue working. Use tenderizer based on your preference.

To tenderize brisket, I like first to rub it with a good amount of The Rub and then use a needle device, then give it a few good smacks with a meat hammer. I am not trying to thin out the brisket, just break up some tissue.

- 5–6 lbs. brisket
- ¼ c. The Rub (p. 181)
- 2 tbsp. Worcestershire
- 1 medium onion, sliced

* Rub the brisket with several dashes of Worcestershire sauce, then apply generous amounts of The Rub. Don't be stingy.
* Place enough aluminum foil down to wrap the brisket. Place sliced onion on the foil. Place brisket on the onion and more sliced onion on the top of the brisket. Wrap the foil around the brisket and onion; seal tightly.
* Place the wrapped brisket in a 14" Dutch oven, placing 10–12 coals on bottom and 14–16 on top. Rotate every 30 minutes and swap out coals as needed to cook for two and a half to three hours.
* Allow to rest for 15 minutes after you remove the heat.
* Slice thin and serve with corn on the cob, bread and butter, some pickles, and BBQ sauce.

Beef Ribs

- 2 racks of beef ribs cut into three rib sections (6–7 lbs.)
- 4 tbsp. The Rub (p. 181)
- 2 tbsp. Worcestershire
- 2 beef bouillon cubes, crushed (or 2 tsp. granules)
- 2 medium onions, sliced into ½" rounds

- After separating the ribs, sprinkle with Worcestershire, bouillon, and The Rub, Massage the ribs with the mix so each is coated.
- Layer sliced onion on bottom of Dutch.
- Place ribs on top of onion.
- Place 14" Dutch oven on 12–14 coals on bottom and 14–16 on top. Rotate every 30 minutes. Swap out coals as needed to cook for 2 hours.
- Serve with a variety of dipping and steak sauces.

Meatloaf/Meatballs

- 4–5 lbs. ground beef (80/20 or 85/15 meat/fat content)
- 2 medium onions, chopped fine
- 2 bell peppers, chopped fine
- 1 c. bread crumbs
- 2 eggs
- ¼ c. Worcestershire
- 3 beef bouillon cubes, crushed fine
- 3 tbsp. Italian Rub (p. 182)
- 2 tbsp. vegetable oil (for the Dutch oven)

* Mix all ingredients, minus the oil, together very well.
* Heat Dutch oven on 16–18 coals and add in 2 tbsp. vegetable oil.
* Form a small amount of the hamburger mix into a silver-dollar-sized hamburger patty.
* Cook it in the Dutch oven and taste it. If your raw hamburger mix needs more flavor, now is the time to add it! Add more Italian Rub or just salt and pepper to taste, then mix.
* For **Meatloaf**, put hamburger mix in oiled Dutch oven, press to a uniform thickness, pull it away from the side about ½" using a spatula, and create a 2" round hole in the center.
* For **Meatballs**, form the meat into uniform balls, about golf-ball size, and layer in the oiled Dutch.
* Place the lid on the oven with 16–18 coals on top, 12–14 coals on the bottom.
* Cook for 1 hour and 30 minutes. Rotate lid and pot one-quarter turn every 15–20 minutes without removing the lid.

Beef Pot Roast

- o   4–5 lbs. beef chuck roast
- o   6–8 medium potatoes, quartered
- o   6 large carrots, quartered
- o   2 medium onions, quartered
- o   4 stalks celery, quartered
- o   3 beef bouillon cubes, crushed
- o   2 tbsp. Worcestershire
- o   1 tbsp. salt
- o   1 tsp. pepper
- o   2 bay leaves
- o   2 c. water
- o   3 tbsp. flour

- Rub roast with Worcestershire and bouillon; place in oiled Dutch oven.
- Add bay leaves and 1 c. water, and then add vegetables.
- Sprinkle salt and pepper over veggies.
- Place lid on oven with 16–18 coals on top, 12–14 coals on bottom.
- Cook for 1 hour and 30 minutes. Rotate lid and pot one-quarter turn every 15–20 minutes without removing the lid.
- At the 1.5-hour mark, mix 1 c. water with 3 tbsp. flour to form a slurry; add to pot, mixing into a broth. (I usually move my veggies to one side, then tilt my Dutch with the lid tool to "pool" the broth so that I can whisk in my slurry mix.)
- Replace lid and cook another 30 minutes.

Italian Beef

- 3–4 lbs. sirloin or round steak
- Juice of 2 limes
- 2 tbsp. Worcestershire
- 3 beef bouillon cubes, crushed
- 2 c. water
- 3 tbsp. Italian Rub (p. 182)
- 2 medium onions, sliced thin
- 2 large bell peppers, sliced thin
- 2 banana peppers, sliced thin
- 2 tbsp. butter
- 1 tsp. salt
- 1 tsp. pepper

- Slice steak diagonally, as thinly as possible.
- Place sliced steak in a ziplock baggie; add Italian Rub, lime juice, and Worcestershire.
- Refrigerate steak for 4–6 hours; remove from fridge 30 minutes before cooking.
- Add butter, salt, pepper, onion, and peppers to Dutch oven atop 20–22 coals.
- Cook 4–5 minutes or until onion becomes slightly translucent.
- Add the steak and cook for an additional 4–5 minutes.
- Add bouillon and water.
- Cover and cook an additional 20–30 minutes.
- Serve on a roll topped with cherry tomatoes and Parmesan. Serve with homemade chips.

Hungarian Goulash (Beef Paprikash)

- 3–4 lbs. stew meat or steak tips (p. 30)
- ⅓ c. olive oil
- 3 onions, sliced
- 2 tbsp. Sweet Hungarian paprika
- 3 tsp. salt
- ½ tsp. pepper
- 1 6 oz. can tomato paste
- 1½ c. water
- 1 clove garlic, crushed and minced

- Place Dutch oven on 16–18 coals.
- Add oil, 1 tsp. salt, and onion; cook until soft. Set onions aside.
- Add beef, remaining salt, pepper, and paprika.
- Cook beef until brown on all sides.
- Add tomato paste, garlic, and water.
- Return onion to Dutch.
- Place lid on oven with 16–18 coals on top, 12–14 coals on the bottom.
- Cook for 2 hours. Rotate lid and pot one-quarter turn every 15–20 minutes without removing the lid.
- Serve over egg noodles or with boiled potatoes and butter.

Beef Tri-Tip Roast

- Two 4- to 5-lb. tri-tip roasts
  - Several sprigs of fresh rosemary (enough for a large handful of leaves)
- ½ c. olive oil
- ¼ c. Worcestershire
- 1 medium onion
- 4 beef bouillon cubes, crushed
- 2 cloves garlic

- Place rosemary leaves, oil, Worcestershire, onion, bouillon cubes, and garlic in your food processor and pulverize. (If you do not have a food processor, chop it all finely—and ask for a food processor for your birthday.)
- Place each roast in a ziplock bag and pour half the mixture into each.
- Refrigerate for 24 hours, remove from fridge, and let stand for 30 minutes before cooking.
- Place your well-oiled Dutch on 22–24 coals; get it hot.
- Brown each roast on both sides for 5 minutes; remove Dutch from heat.
- Add both roasts to Dutch oven and salt.
- Place lid on oven with 18–20 coals on top, 14–16 coals on bottom.
- Cook for 20–30 minutes or until desired internal temperature is reached (You can use a thermometer. I prefer rare at 130°.)
- Let roasts stand for 10 minutes before slicing.

Barbacoa de Res (Beef BBQ Mexican Style)

- 4–5 lbs. chuck roast
- 2 tbsp. olive oil
- 4 bay leaves
- 3 tbsp. Mexican Rub (p. 180)
- ⅓ c. cider vinegar
- ½ c. beef broth
- 3 garlic cloves, crushed and minced
- 1 bouillon cube, crushed
- 3 limes, juiced
- 3–4 chipotle chiles, canned in adobo

* Warm a 14" Dutch on 22–24 coals; add oil.
* Rub bouillon and lime juice into roast; brown for 2–3 minutes on each side.
* Blend remaining ingredients or chop them fine; mix together into a slurry and pour over roast.
* Place lid on oven with 16–18 coals on top, 12–14 coals on the bottom.
* Cook for 2-hours and 30–45 minutes. Rotate lid and pot one-quarter turn every 15–20 minutes without removing the lid.
* Shred meat and enjoy with tortillas or gorditas (p. 94) and rice and beans.

5 Chicken

Introduction

Chicken is a dangerous beast. This one time at Dutch-oven camp, a good friend of mine cooked up a batch of chicken breasts and forgot about them, as we Dutchers tend to do. By the time we returned to remove the lid from the Dutch, the chicken had sucked dry all the moisture from the western part of Utah.

Boneless, skinless white meat is healthy but can get rubbery and dry if cooked using the same methods as dark meat. My recipes typically call for legs and thighs because they are far more forgiving when it comes to heat and cooking duration. Leg quarters are a great value as well, costing quite a bit less than boneless, skinless options. The leg quarters also make it easy to gauge serving sizes for large groups of people.

White meat is the new vegetable, at least at my house. Nothing goes better with steak and potatoes than a grilled chicken breast covered in ham and Swiss cheese, two more of my favorite vegetables. OK, seriously, I will give you a few recipes with boneless, skinless breasts as the ingredient. By learning the technique for cooking them without overcooking them, you can skew any recipe to fit. You can always cut out the butter and add a butter alternative (think flavor). Oils can be substituted as long as you use an oil that is comfortable with the temperature you are cooking at. Be careful with olive oil; do not get it too hot, or it will smoke and taste burnt.

Most of the recipes in this section call for the same type and amount of chicken. I want to highlight how easy it is to change methods. Usually, with one or two different spices and a sauce choice, you can create an entirely new meal. The benefit is that you become very familiar with the Dutch-oven cooking steps.

Now, remember your coal preparation!

Cilantro Lime Chicken

- 8 chicken quarters (to be separated into legs and thighs)
- 3 whole limes
- 1 stick butter, 8 tbsp.
- 1 bunch cilantro
- 1 medium onion
- 1 tsp. pepper (or to taste)
- 1 tbsp. seasoned salt (or to taste)
- ¼ c. vegetable oil

- Separate quarters into legs and thighs; salt and pepper the chicken.
- Pull leaves from cilantro sprigs; chop fine.
- Zest limes, set limes aside.
- Mix lime zest, butter, and cilantro until soft.
- Using your fingers, stuff a bit of butter underneath the skin of each chicken piece.
- Pour vegetable oil in Dutch oven.
- Slice onion into six rounds, breaking apart to layer half in the Dutch oven.
- Place chicken in Dutch on top of onion; place the other half of onions over chicken.
- Squeeze limes over onion and chicken; add salt and pepper.
- Place lid on oven with 16–18 coals on top, 12–14 on the bottom.
- Cook for 1 hour and 30 minutes. Rotate lid and pot one-quarter turn every 15–20 minutes without removing the lid.
- Serve with white or brown rice, green beans, or broccoli.

BBQ Chicken

- 8 chicken quarters (to be separated into legs and thighs)
- 2 c. Best BBQ Sauce Ever! (p. 177)
- 1 stick butter, 8 tbsp.
    - Omit butter if desired
- 1 medium onion
- 1 large bell pepper
- 4 tbsp. The Rub (p. 181)
- ¼ c. vegetable oil

- Separate quarters into legs and thighs.
- Season the chicken liberally with The Rub.
- Pour vegetable oil into the Dutch oven.
- Slice onion into six rounds; break rounds apart and layer half in the Dutch oven.
- Place the chicken in the Dutch on top of onion; place the other half of onions over chicken.
- Slice butter into small pats; place around onion.
- Pour sauce over chicken.
- Place lid on oven with 16–18 coals on top, 12–14 on the bottom.
- Cook for 1 hour and 15–30 minutes. Rotate lid and pot one-quarter turn every 15–20 minutes without removing the lid.
- When chicken is cooked, thicken the sauce by removing the chicken from the Dutch, placing all coals on the bottom, and bringing the sauce to a light boil until reduced by half.
- Serve with coleslaw (p. 146).

Sweet and Sour

- 8 chicken quarters (to be separated into legs and thighs)
- 2 c. Sweet 'n Sour to Die For (p. 178)
- 1 medium onion
- 1 large bell pepper
- 1 tsp. pepper
- 1 tbsp. seasoned salt
- 1 tsp. ground ginger

- Separate quarters into legs and thighs.
- Season chicken with ginger, salt, and pepper.
- Slice onion into six rounds; break rounds apart and layer half in the Dutch oven.
- Slice bell pepper into ¼"-thick strips.
- Place chicken in Dutch on top of onion; place the other half of onions and all bell peppers over the chicken; pour sauce over chicken.
- Place lid on oven with 16–18 coals on top, 12–14 on the bottom.
- Cook for 1 hour and 15–30 minutes. Rotate lid and pot one-quarter turn every 15–20 minutes without removing the lid,
- When chicken is cooked, thicken the sauce by removing chicken from the Dutch, placing all coals on the bottom, and bringing sauce to a light boil until reduced by half.
- Serve with white or brown rice or Dutch fried rice (p. 147).

Roast Chicken

- o 2 whole chickens
- o 2 medium onions, sliced
- o ¼ c. olive oil
- o 3 tbsp. Italian Rub (p. 182)

- Using kitchen shears or a knife, remove the backbone of the chicken and press halves flat, breast side up. It is as easy as cutting down either side of the backbone.
- Rub chicken lightly with half of the olive oil.
- Pour the other half of the oil into the bottom of the Dutch oven.
- Place sliced onion in bottom of Dutch.
- Rub chickens with the Italian Rub.
- Place chicken halves in the Dutch oven, flat and breast side up. If needed, cut chickens into halves or quarters. Keep as much skin facing up and exposed as possible.
- Place lid on oven with 16–18 coals on top, 12–14 on the bottom.
- Cook for 1 hour and 30 minutes. Rotate lid and pot one-quarter turn every 15–20 minutes without removing the lid.
- Serve with Cheesy Potatoes (p. 139).

"Wade, I can't help but notice that you put onion slices under all chicken recipes."

Yes, I do! Onion infuses the chicken with a sweet flavor. Feel free to omit them if you are not an onion fan, but I encourage you to try it.

Garlic and Butter Chicken

- 8 large chicken breasts
- 4 cloves of garlic (big cloves)
- 1 stick butter, 8 tbsp.
- 2 tbsp. seasoned salt (or to taste)
- 1 tsp. pepper (or to taste)
- 1 medium onion
- 2 tbsp. vegetable oil

- Crush and mince garlic; mix with a fork into butter until soft.
- Place breasts flat on a sturdy surface and lightly pound them until they are of uniform thickness (about ¾" thick). Season each side of each breast with salt and pepper.
- Place Dutch oven on 20–22 coals and let it get warm (2–3 minutes).
- Put a small amount of vegetable oil (about 1 tbsp.) in the Dutch.

- Sear each breast 2–3 minutes on each side; set aside.
- Cut onion into six rounds; place half on the bottom of the Dutch.
- Place breasts on onion in Dutch, and pat each piece with a dab of garlic-butter mix.
- Place remaining onion on top; add remaining oil and garlic butter.
- Place lid on oven with 16–18 coals on top, 12–14 on the bottom.

- Cook for an additional 20–25 minutes. Rotate lid and pot one-quarter turn every 15–20 minutes. (Do not overcook, please.)
- Serve with Italian Roasted Potatoes (p. 140) or rice.
- This dish goes great with any of your favorite sauces. The Sweet 'n Sour (p. 178) is awesome on this.

Did you know that an inexpensive tote that's large enough to hold your Dutch-oven tools can be inverted and used as a small prep surface when you're out camping? I store my lighter, gloves, utensils, lid tool, tongs, and other small items in a tote that makes a great little table. A flexible chopping mat makes a wonderful "tote table cloth" and an easy-to-clean prep surface.

Teriyaki Chicken

- 8 chicken quarters (to be separated into legs and thighs)
- 2 c. Tenacious Teriyaki Sauce (p. 179)
- 1 medium onion
- 1 large bell pepper
- 2 large carrots, chopped
- 1 tsp. pepper
- 1 tbsp. seasoned salt
- 1 tsp. ground ginger or 2 tsp. fresh

- Season chicken with ginger, salt, and pepper.
- Slice onion into six rounds; break apart and layer half in the Dutch oven.
- Add chopped carrots.
- Slice bell pepper into ¼"-thick strips.
- Place chicken in the Dutch on top of onion; place the other half of onions and all bell peppers over the chicken. Pour the sauce over the chicken.
- Place lid on oven with 16–18 coals on top, 12–14 on the bottom.
- Cook for 1 hour and 20 minutes. Rotate lid and pot one-quarter turn every 15–20 minutes without removing the lid.
- When chicken is cooked, thicken sauce by removing chicken from the Dutch, placing all coals on the bottom, and bringing the sauce to a light boil until reduced by half.
- Serve with white or brown rice or Dutch Fried Rice (p. 147).

Tandoori Chicken in the Dutch

- 8 chicken quarters (to be separated into legs and thighs)
- 1 c. plain yogurt
- 1 tbsp. lime juice
- 1 tsp. ground ginger
- 1 tsp. paprika
- 1 tsp. allspice, ground
- 1 tsp. pepper
- 1 tsp. ground cayenne
- 1 tsp. cinnamon
- 2 tsp. cumin
- 2 tsp. seasoned salt
- 4 cloves garlic, finely minced
- 1 tbsp. chili paste (Thai works great.)
- 1 medium onion, sliced
- 1 tbsp. vegetable oil

* Mix yogurt, lime juice, and all the spices into a thick marinade.
* Cover chicken in marinade. (Ziplock bags work great for this.)
* Refrigerate for 12–24 hours.
* Remove the chicken from refrigerator 20 minutes before cooking.
* Place Dutch oven on 14–16 coals; add oil and sliced onion.
* Layer chicken in Dutch; use marinade to cover any naked spots on chicken.
* Add remaining marinade to top.

- Place lid on oven with 16–18 coals on top.
- Cook for 1 hour and 20 minutes. Rotate lid and pot one-quarter turn every 15–20 minutes without removing the lid.
- Let chicken rest in the oven for an additional 15 minutes when cooking is done.
- Serve with jasmine rice and flat bread (p. 84).

Chicken Fingers
- 4 boneless, skinless chicken breasts
- 1 batch beer batter breading (p. 90)
- 1 tbsp. seasoned salt
- 2 qts. vegetable or peanut oil

- Slice chicken into 1"-wide fingers.
- Season with salt.
- Prepare a 14" Dutch on top of 30–32 coals, or use burner to bring oil temperature to 375°F–400°F; use a thermometer, and keep the oil in this range.
- Dip the strips into the batter and fry for 4–5 minutes.
- Drain on a rack to avoid oil puddles.
- Serve warm with Cheesy Biscuits (p. 89).

Fried Chicken

- 8 chicken quarters (to be separated into legs and thighs)
- 4 tbsp. The Rub (p. 181)
- 2 c. flour (for dredging)
- 2 c. buttermilk
- Dash of hot sauce (1 dash good, 2 dashes better, 3 dashes…and so on)
- Enough oil or shortening to fill the Dutch oven one-third full

- Marinate chicken 12–24 hours, refrigerated, in buttermilk and hot sauce.
- Heat oil in Dutch atop 28–30 coals to get the temp to 350°F. Keep the temperature in the 350°F range.
- Drain the chicken of marinade.
- Liberally season the chicken with The Rub; mix any remaining Rub into the flour
- Dredge the chicken in flour and shake off the excess.
- Cook the chicken in heated oil until golden brown, 10–12 minutes per side.
- Watch your temperature; use a thermometer.
- Use a rack to drain the chicken pieces.
- Serve with coleslaw (p. 146).

Chicken and Dumplings

- 6 chicken quarters (to be separated into legs and thighs)
- 3 c. baking mix (p. 89)
- 1½ c. buttermilk
- 3 carrots, chopped
- 2 celery stalks, chopped
- 4–6 medium potatoes, into 2" cubes
- 1 medium onion, chopped
- 2 bay leaves
- 1 c. peas (Frozen peas are fine.)
- 2 tsp. poultry seasoning
- 1 tbsp. seasoned salt
- 1 tsp. pepper
- 1 tbsp. olive oil
- 1 tbsp. butter
- ⅓ c. flour
- 6 c. chicken stock

- Place Dutch oven over 20–22 coals and heat butter and oil for 2–3 minutes.
- Season chicken with seasoned salt and pepper.
- Add vegetables, bay leaves, salt, pepper, and poultry seasoning.
- Add the chicken; stir to mix. (Stir occasionally; you want some brown sticky on the bottom of the Dutch.)
- Cook for 5–6 minutes.

- Add the flour to the pan; cook 2 more minutes while stirring.

- Add the broth and bring to a boil; disturb the brown sticky on the bottom of the Dutch.

- Place lid on oven with 16–18 coals on top, 12–14 on the bottom.

- Cook for 40 minutes. Rotate lid and pot one-quarter turn every 20 minutes without removing the lid.

- In a bowl, combine baking mix and buttermilk. (Biscuits work great, too, canned or the homemade recipe on p. 86.)

- Form dough into 3" round, 1" thick biscuits and place evenly around the top of the chicken. I use two spoons to create the dumplings.

- Place lid on the oven with 16–18 coals on top, 12–14 on the bottom.

- Cook for an additional 30 minutes. Rotate lid and pot one-quarter turn every 15 minutes without removing the lid.

Spice Is Nice Chicken

- 6–8 boneless, skinless chicken breasts
- Juice of 2 limes
- 3 tbsp. The Rub (p. 181)
- 1 tbsp. olive oil
- 2 tbsp. Worcestershire

- Lightly pound chicken with a meat hammer to uniform thickness, ¾".
- Place flattened breasts equally into two gallon-size ziplock bags.
- Mix all other ingredients in a small bowl, adding half to each bag of breasts.
- Zip bags, pressing out all air.
- Flatten the meat in the bags as much as possible; massage marinade into the chicken.
- Refrigerate overnight.
- Remove bags from refrigerator 20 minutes before cooking.
- Heat Dutch oven on 20–22 coals.
- Cook each breast 3 minutes on each side (usually two at a time).
- When finished, return all breasts to the Dutch.
- Cook on top of 12–14 coals bottom, 16–18 coals on top for 20–25 minutes or until juices run clear.
- For a complete and healthy meal, add three heads of fresh broccoli, a squeeze of lime each, and a dash of salt before putting the lid on.

Chicken Fajitas

- 4–6 chicken breasts, sliced into fajita strips about 3" long and 1" wide
- 2 medium onions, sliced into rings and then halved
- 3 medium bell peppers, sliced into rings and then halved (Use various colors.)
- 3 tbsp. Mexican Rub (p. 180)
- 2 tsp. seasoned salt
- 2 tbsp. vegetable oil
- 2 dozen corn tortillas

- Heat a 14" Dutch on 22–24 coals; heat lid on 14 coals upside down for cooking.
- Add oil to Dutch; season chicken with seasoned salt.
- Cook chicken strips 2–4 minutes to brown.
- Add onion, peppers, and Mexican Rub.
- Cook while stirring for another 13–15 minutes or until done.
- On the lid, warm corn tortillas 4–5 at a time; wrap in paper towels.
- Serve fajitas hot from the Dutch with warm tortillas and your favorite condiments.

Tasty Tidbit: Here's how to make a great casserole. After adding onion and peppers, add two 14-oz. cans of enchilada sauce and cover the mix with half a batch of cornbread (p. 93). Cook with 12–14 coals on bottom and 16–18 coals on top for 30–40 minutes.

6 Pork

A Pig's Tale

When I was five years old, I would travel with my father to the cotton gin. I was amazed and entranced by the giant vacuum that sucked the fluffy, fuzzy white cotton from the trailer. The gentleman running the machine would hand my dad a weight receipt when he was done. Dad and I would take this receipt to the gin office and turn it in for an accounting.

One day as we were leaving the office, I noticed the man open a door to the back room. He handed the receipt to a pig wearing glasses and sitting at a desk running an old Monroe rotary calculator. I tugged at Dad, but he was too slow to see what I had seen before the door closed. The man winked at me, and we left.

The next day, we returned with another load of cotton, and again we arrived at the gin office for our accounting. As we left, I watched closely as Dad led me from the building. Sure enough, the door opened, and there sat the same pig, calculating with the old Monroe rotary calculator. This time, the pig was bandaged, and it appeared that one leg was missing, all the way to the hip. Again, I pleaded with Dad to look, but to no satisfaction, he was busy talking business with another farmer.

A few days later, my father took me along to the gin again, and again I found myself in the office waiting for the door to open so I could see the pig accountant. To my great relief, the door opened, and there sat the pig. This time, he was missing both legs and bandaged to the waist. Luckily, my father saw it.

"Hey!" Dad screamed. "Is that a pig doing your accounting?"

The man calmly turned around and looked at the pig, who regarded him in return before the door closed. "Yep, sure is," he replied slowly and with little concern for the question, all the while looking at his desk and a newspaper he attempted to read.

"Well, I'll be." Dad slapped at his leg as if to show his disbelief in the most amazing thing he had ever seen. "That is the dadgummist thing I have ever seen. It's a miracle!"

"Yep," the man answered, starting to show his irritation with the line of conversation and distraction from his newspaper.

"Let me ask you, though," Dad inquired. "What the heck happened to his legs? That must have been a heck of an accident."

The man looked up from his desk and paper and said calmly and with a flat tone, "An intelligent pig like that you don't eat all at once."

Did you know that lid cooking requires a lot more heat? You will need a blanket of coals, 24–26, for a 14" lid. Remember, coals need air to burn and maintain heat, so lift the lid just above the coals with a few rocks placed around the edges.

Introduction

Similar to beef sirloin, pork can be prepared effortlessly for multiple recipes with a single method. You can add sauces and spices easily on the second cooking to change the flavor completely. The first method shows basic pork loin tips that can be made into several different entrees—pork loin sliced into chops and then cubed or boneless pork chops work great. Bone-in chops also work but require a tad more knife work and trimming.

Pork Loin Tips

- 4–5 lbs. pork loin or boneless chops, cubed to 2" x 2" (give or take 25 percent)
- 2 tsp. seasoned salt
- 1 tsp. pepper
- ½ tsp. garlic powder
- 1 tsp. onion powder
- 2 tbsp. Worcestershire
- ½ tsp. thyme, ground

- Place well-oiled Dutch on 24–26 coals; add all ingredients.
- Brown for 5 minutes, and then follow directions for the recipe you want to make.

You can make several different meals. Which one you choose will determine what you do next. A couple of decisions need to be made now. What will your sides be? Where do you want your flavor profile to go? If you want to, you can continue cooking for 20 minutes or until the desired doneness is reached. I recommend that you read on. The following pages contain some "saucy" ideas.

Souvlaki

- 1 batch pork loin tips (p. 66)
- 1 medium onion, sliced thin and chopped into quarters
- Greek Sauce (p. 176). Or you can use 2 tbsp. of your favorite Greek seasoning and the juice of 4 limes.

• Place Dutch oven on 24–26 coals. We want to fry, so we are looking for 350°F.

• Add onion to loin tips; cook for 5 minutes or until onions start to caramelize.

• Add sauce to browned pork; stir to mix.

• Simmer for 20–25 minutes or until sauce has reduced by half.

• Serve with lemon rice (p. 149), flat bread (p. 84), and tzatziki (p. 179).

BBQ Pork Loin Tips

- 1 batch pork loin tips (p. 66)
- 2 c. Best BBQ Sauce Ever! (p.177) (Or you can use 2 c. of your favorite BBQ sauce. Add ½ tsp. ground cayenne or crushed red flakes for extra spice. Or try 1 tsp. of your favorite hot sauce for a variation.)

- Add the sauce and 1 stick butter to browned pork loin; stir to mix. (For variety, add chopped bell peppers when you add the sauce.)
- Place Dutch oven on 24–26 coals; we are looking for 350°F.
- Simmer for 20–25 minutes or until sauce has reduced by one-third.
- Serve on a roll, over white or brown rice, or on top of a baked potato.

Green Chile

- 1 batch pork loin tips (p. 66)
- 2 4-oz. cans diced green chiles
- 1 28-oz. can enchilada sauce
- 2 medium onions, chopped coarsely
- 1 tbsp. cumin
- 1 tbsp. Mexican oregano
- Juice of 3 limes

- Mix all ingredients together in the Dutch.
- Place lid on the oven with 16–18 coals on top, 10–12 on the bottom.
- Cook for 1 hour. Rotate lid and pot one-quarter turn every 15–20 minutes without removing the lid.
- Serve with Spanish Rice (p. 148) and/or on tortillas, either flour or corn, with sliced onion, radish, cilantro, and your favorite salsa.

Sweet and Sour Pork

- 1 batch pork loin tips (p. 66)
- 1 c. Sweet 'n Sour to Die For (p. 178) or 1 c. of your favorite sweet 'n sour sauce
- ½ c. pineapple juice
- 1 medium onion
- 1 large bell pepper
- 1 tsp. pepper
- ½ tsp. seasoned salt
- 2 tsp. ground ginger
- 2 tbsp. cornstarch

* Season browned pork loin with ginger, salt, and pepper.
* Mix cornstarch in pineapple juice; mix with Sweet and Sour sauce.
* Slice onion into six rounds. Break rounds apart and layer half in the Dutch oven.
* Slice bell pepper into ¼"-thick strips.
* Add pork loin to Dutch on top of onion; place the other half of onions and all bell peppers over pork. Pour sauce mix over all.
* Place lid on the oven with 16–18 coals on top, 10–12 on the bottom.
* Cook for 1 hour. Rotate lid and pot one-quarter turn every 15–20 minutes without removing the lid.
* Serve with white or brown rice, or make some Dutch Fried Rice (p. 147).

Teriyaki Pork

- o   1 batch pork loin tips (p. 66)
- o   2 c. Tenacious Teriyaki Sauce (p. 179) or substitute 2 c. of your favorite teriyaki sauce

- Add sauce and 1 stick butter to browned pork loin; stir to mix.
- Place Dutch oven on 24–26 coals; we are looking for 350°F.
- Simmer for 20–25 minutes or until sauce has reduced by one-third.
- Serve over white or brown rice, with fried rice, or with a baked potato.

Did you know that you can preheat your Dutch as you light your coals by setting the chimney on top of the lid?

Pork and Apples

- 1 batch pork loin tips (p. 66)
- 4–5 medium apples, skinned, cored, and chopped
- 2 large onions, chopped
- 2 tsp. cinnamon
- 1 tsp. ground cayenne
- ½ c. apple cider
- 1 tbsp. cornstarch

- Mix cornstarch with apple juice.
- Add ingredients to prepared pork loin; stir to mix.
- Place lid on oven with 16–18 coals on top, 12 coals on bottom.
- Cook for 1 hour. Rotate lid and pot one-quarter turn every 15–20 minutes without removing the lid.
- Serve over white or brown rice or with a baked potato.

Carnitas

- 1 batch pork loin tips (p. 66)
- 1 tbsp. cumin
- 1 tbsp. Mexican oregano
- 2 tsp. cinnamon
- 1 tsp. ground cayenne
- ½ lb. bacon, cooked and chopped
- 1 large onion, chopped coarsely

- Add bacon and spices to cube mix; cook for 5 minutes, stirring as needed.
- Place lid on oven with 14–16 coals on top, 12–14 on the bottom.
- Cook for 1 hour. Rotate lid and pot one-quarter turn every 15–20 minutes without removing the lid.
- Serve on tortillas, either flour or corn, with sliced onion, radish, cilantro, or your favorite salsa.

Pork Schnitzel

- 8 pork rib or loin chops, ½" thick, boneless
- Breading mix:
    - 1 c. cornmeal
    - 1 c. flour
    - 2 tbsp. seasoned salt
    - 2 tbsp. ground sage
    - 1 tbsp. onion powder
    - 2 tbsp. paprika
- Enough vegetable oil to fill the Dutch oven one-third full (2 qts.)
- 2 c. buttermilk
- 2 tbsp. hot sauce

- In a container or ziplock bag, mix buttermilk and hot sauce.
- Marinate chops for 2–4 hours in buttermilk and hot sauce.
- Prepare breading mix in a small tray.
- Shake each chop so it is not dripping; then press into dry mix on both sides.
- Bring the oil in Dutch oven to 350°F (use a thermometer) on top of 26–28 coals.
- One by one, fry each chop for 4–5 minutes a side or until golden brown and juices run clear.
- Serve with German Potato Salad (p. 145).

Let us have a moment of silence for the majestic Pork Schnitzel….

Pork Picnic

- 7–8 lbs. pork picnic (pork shoulder)
- ⅓ c. The Rub (p. 181)
- 1 tbsp. seasoned salt
- 2 tbsp. Worcestershire

- Rub the shoulder with several dashes of Worcestershire sauce. Apply a generous amount of The Rub and 1 tbsp. seasoned salt. Don't be stingy—get under the skin and in the natural separations of the muscle.
- Place the shoulder, fattiest side up, in a 14" Dutch oven. Place 10–12 coals on bottom and 14–16 on top. The Minion Method works great here (p. 19–20).
- Cook for 3 hours. Rotate lid and pot one-quarter turn every 30 minutes without removing the lid.
- Allow to rest for 15–30 minutes after you remove from heat.
- Tear apart or shred, season as needed, and serve with corn on the cob, bread and butter, some pickles, and BBQ sauce.

Pork Ribs

- 4–5 lbs. pork ribs (St. Louis or baby back)
- ¼ c. The Rub (p. 181)
- 2 tbsp. Worcestershire
- 2 c. Best BBQ Sauce Ever! (p. 177)

• Cut ribs into three to four sections.

• Rub the ribs with several dashes of Worcestershire sauce; apply generous amounts of The Rub. Don't be stingy.

• Place the ribs in a 14" Dutch oven, with 10–12 coals on bottom and 12–14 on top.

• Cook for 2 hours. Rotate lid and pot one-quarter turn every 30 minutes without removing the lid.

• Add sauce over the top; cook an additional 30 minutes.

• Allow to rest for 15–30 minutes after you remove the ribs from the heat.

• Serve with coleslaw (p. 146) and baked beans (p. 150).

Roast Pork Chops in the Dutch

- 6–8 boneless pork chops, ¾" to 1" thick
- Juice of 2 limes
- 3 tbsp. Italian Rub (p. 182)
- ½ tsp. ground sage
- 1 tbsp. olive oil
- 2 tbsp. Worcestershire

- Place equal portions of chops into two gallon-size ziplock bags.
- Mix all other ingredients in a small bowl; add half to each bag of chops.
- Zip bags and press out all air.
- Flatten meat in the bags as much as possible; massage marinade into the pork.
- Refrigerate overnight; remove bags from refrigerator 20 minutes before cooking.
- Heat Dutch oven on 26–28 coals.
- Cook chops for 3 minutes on each side (usually two at a time).
- When finished, add all chops back into the Dutch.
- Cook on top of coals: 12–14 on bottom, 16–18 on top, for 30 minutes.

Did you know that you can use just about any 14- to 16-oz. bag of frozen vegetables and have a great-tasting side dish? Add 2 tbsp. lime juice, 1 tbsp. olive oil, 1 tsp. seasoned salt, and ½ tsp. pepper to your vegetables. Cook in the Dutch with 20 coals on bottom and 10 coals on top for 15 minutes.

7 Bread

The bread recipe that follows was handed down from my great-great-great-great-grandmother O'Cedar Rider. Grams lived in the small village of Amathotown in a home owned by the Parker family.

It is rumored that Grandma O'Cedar was a witch. She spent quite a bit of time alone, tending to her home and baking. Tale tells it she was never seen without her broom. It seemed that no one in her village liked her; in fact, most were afraid of her and her broom.

Her sister, Ira, who most found annoying at best, married a baker—a terrible baker by the name of Tatum. The pair was in a dire financial way and about to go belly up because his baking was so bad. After several sibling squabbles, Ira stole her sister's recipes and made up some elaborate story about how the dough was plagued, and Grams O'Cedar was burned at the stake.

With her last breath, she cursed our family, and that is why it is said that, to this day, we all crave hot-'n-spicy food and reek of charcoal.

By no small coincidence, after my mother and father were married, my father would brag on his brother's cornbread. With each meal, as Mom made the cornbread, she would alter and work to make is sweeter and fluffier, lighter, and more buttery. With each meal, the cornbread quickly approached perfection. However, much to her dismay, at each meal, Father would announce how great his brother's cornbread was.

Finally in a fit of frustration, and rightfully so, Mother yelled, "What was so danged great about his cornbread!"

Father turned calmly and replied with his thumb and forefinger pinched closely together for her to see: "It was about this thin and burnt to a crisp."

The Only Recipe You Will Ever Knead

- 2 tbsp. active dry yeast
- ¾ c. warm water (110°F)
- ⅔ c. sugar
- 2 eggs, beaten
- 2 c. warm canned milk (110°F)
- 1 cube butter, melted
- 1 tbsp. salt
- 8 c. flour (plus extra for kneading)
- A spritz of vegetable or olive oil

- Mix warm water and 1 tbsp. sugar and yeast; set aside for 5–8 minutes.
- Mix remaining sugar, milk, salt, butter, and eggs in a large bowl.
- Mix yeast with wet ingredients; begin adding flour until you can't mix by hand.
- Turn onto a properly floured kneading surface and work in remaining flour; knead vigorously for 5–8 minutes.
- Return to bowl and spritz top with vegetable oil. Cover with plastic wrap and a towel to keep warm; place in a warm spot.
- Allow to double in size.

- Now you can cut into rolls, half into loaves, roll into pizza crusts, roll out cinnamon rolls, or make *zombie buns*! The dough is multipurpose and super yummy.

Did you know that kids and adults like cutting and shaping dough into freaky shapes and creatures? Mix up a batch of dough and give equal amounts to a party of youth. Let them get creative while you warm up a couple of ovens. You can cook five or six "dough creatures" in each oven!

Parker House Rolls

- o   1 batch TORYWEK (That's an ancient Nordic term for bread dough, p. 81)
- o   ½ stick butter, melted

- Roll dough out until it's 1" thick.
- Use a biscuit cutter or large glass to create "rounds" about 4" across.
- With a butter knife, make an indention in the center to keep rolls from opening during cooking.
- Brush with butter and fold in half; brush top with butter.
- Allow to rise for 15 minutes in a warm place (90°F–110°F).
- Place lid on Dutch, 18 coals on top, 10 on the bottom.
- Cook for 20 minutes. Rotate lid and oven one-quarter turn after 10 minutes without lifting lid.

You can use your Dutch oven to make your buns and rolls rise. Place 1 coal at the center and 4 coals at the outer edges, equally spaced on the bottom. Place 1 coal at the center and 4 coals on the lid at the outer edge, equally spaced but offset from the bottom coals.

Dinner Rolls

- Roll TORYWEK (p. 81) to 2" thick; cut into 3" x 3" squares.
- Allow to rise for 15 minutes in a warm place (90°F–110°F).
- Place lid on Dutch, 18 coals on top, 10 on the bottom.
- Cook for 20 minutes. Rotate lid and oven one-quarter turn after 10 minutes without lifting lid.

Sandwich Rolls

- Roll TORYWEK (p. 81) out to 2" thick; cut into 3" x 5" rectangles.
- Allow to rise for 15 minutes in a warm place (90°F–110°F).
- Place lid on Dutch, 18 coals on top, 10 on the bottom.
- Cook for 20–25 minutes. Rotate lid and oven one-quarter turn after 10 minutes without lifting lid.

Flat Bread

- Roll TORYWEK (p. 81) into a 3" log shape.
- Slice 2" rounds off of dough log.
- Use your palm to flatten to ½" thick and form into 6" rounds (flat bread shapes).
- Allow to rest for 15 minutes; do not stack.
- Place Dutch on 24–26 coals. Add 1 tbsp. vegetable oil; smear oil around evenly.
- Cook flat breads 4–5 minutes per side or until golden brown.

Savory Rolls

- 1 batch TORYWEK (p. 81)
- 2 sticks butter
- 1 bunch fresh rosemary (about 2 tbsp. chopped)
- 1 bunch fresh thyme (about 2 tbsp. chopped)
- 2 cloves garlic, crushed and minced fine
- 1 tsp. pepper

- Mix butter, pepper, and herbs with garlic and set aside. (You just made a compound butter.) Do this the night before and place in the fridge in a ziplock baggie. Remove from the refrigerator 1 hour before cooking to soften. You can also store this compound butter mixture in the fridge for use on toast, biscuits, pizza dough, or on meats such as chicken and steak.
- Roll out TORYWEK as if you were making cinnamon rolls, about ½" thick. I prefer to make a square about 24" x 24" x ½".
- Spread softened compound butter evenly across the dough.
- Roll into a log (just like making cinnamon rolls) as tightly as you can without crushing the dough.
- Cut into 1"-thick rounds.
- Place rolls evenly and touching lightly in the bottom of a lightly greased 14" Dutch.
- Place lid on the Dutch with 18 coals on top, 10 on the bottom.
- Cook for 20 minutes. Rotating lid and oven one-quarter turn after 10 minutes without lifting lid.

Biscuits

- o 2 c. flour
- o 2 tsp. baking powder
- o 1 tsp. salt
- o ½ c. butter (cold)
- o 1 c. buttermilk

- Mix flour, baking powder, and salt.
- Cube butter into ¼" chunks.
- Combine flour mix and butter together with a fork until small, pea-like pellets form.
- Add the buttermilk slowly to make a soft ball.
- Roll the dough onto a floured surface until ½" thick; cut into biscuits (rounds or squares).
- Place biscuits evenly and touching lightly in the bottom of a lightly greased 14" Dutch.
- Place lid on the Dutch with 18 coals on top, 10 on the bottom.
- Cook for 20–25 minutes. Rotate lid and oven one-quarter turn after 10 minutes without lifting lid.

Sourdough Biscuits

- 1 tsp. salt
- 2 c. flour
- 2 tsp. baking powder
- ½ c. butter (cold)
- 2 c. sourdough starter (p. 95)
- 1 tbsp. warm water (if needed)

- Mix flour, baking powder, and salt.
- Cube butter into ¼" chunks.
- Mix flour mix and butter together with a fork until small, pea-like pellets form.
- Add sourdough starter to make a soft ball of dough. Your starter consistency determines how much water and flour are required. If the dough feels too dry, add warm water 1 tbsp. at a time until desired consistency is reached. If dough feels too moist, add flour 1 tbsp. at a time until desired consistency is reached.
- Roll dough onto a floured surface until ½ thick; cut into biscuits (rounds or squares).
- Place biscuits evenly and touching lightly in the bottom of a lightly greased 14" Dutch.
- Place lid on the Dutch with 18 coals on top, 10 on the bottom.
- Cook for 15–20 minutes. Rotate lid and oven one-quarter turn after 10 minutes without lifting lid.

Traditional Fry Bread

- 4 c. flour
- 2 tbsp. baking powder
- 1 tsp. salt
- 1 c. water
- ½ c. lard (or shortening) for mix
- 3 c. lard (or shortening) for frying

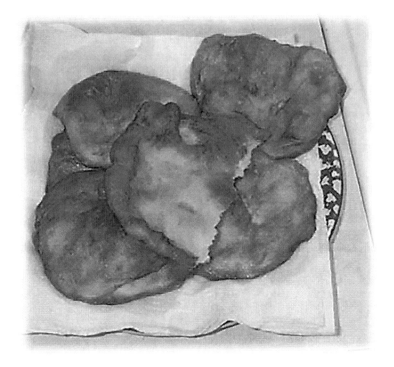

- Mix flour, salt, and baking powder.
- Mix in ½ c. lard and 1 c. water.
- Mix thoroughly until dough is soft and not sticky.
- Roll into 3" balls.
- In a Dutch oven on top of 26–28 coals, heat remaining lard to 350°F.
- Using your palms, flatten dough balls into round fry-bread shape. Thickness is according to preference, but thinner is better.
- Gently place dough into hot oil and cook one at a time.
- Cook to golden brown (2–3 minutes per side).
- For a sweet treat, dust with powdered sugar or spread with honey butter or butter and jam.
- Or top with chili, onion, sour cream, salsa, and jalapeños for a great Navajo taco.

Baking Mix

- 6 c. flour
- 3 tbsp. baking powder
- 1 tbsp. salt
- 1 c. butter-flavored shortening

- Sift dry ingredients together three or four times.
- Cut in shortening until mixed completely.
- Store refrigerated and airtight. Mix will survive a week of camping unrefrigerated.
- Use whenever "baking mix" is called for.

Cheesy Biscuits

- 3 c. baking mix (p. 89)
- 1⅓ c. buttermilk
- 2 c. cheese, shredded

- Mix all ingredients together.
- Spoon 3" dollops into a well-oiled 14" Dutch.
- Place biscuits evenly and touching lightly in the bottom of a lightly greased 14" Dutch.
- Place lid on the Dutch with 18 coals on top, 10 on the bottom.
- Cook for 15–20 minutes. Rotate lid and oven one-quarter turn after 10 minutes without lifting lid.

Pie Crust

- o 2 c. flour
- o 1 stick butter-flavored shortening, approximately 8 tbsp. (cold)
- o 2 tsp. salt
- o 1 small bowl ice water

- Cut shortening into flour and salt until small, pea-like granules form.
- Add 1 tbsp. of ice water at a time until dough comes together (about 4 tbsp.).
- Wrap in cellophane; refrigerate for at least 1 hour.
- Roll out thin for two pie crusts.

Beer Batter Breading

- o 2 c. flour
- o ½ c. cornstarch
- o 1 tbsp. baking powder
- o 16 oz. dark beer (If you have no beer, use half water and half buttermilk or try ginger-beer.)

- Mix together to form a smooth batter.
- Great for onion, zucchini, and mushrooms.

Pizza

- ½ batch TORYWEK (p. 81, or a can of dough works)
- 3 c. mozzarella cheese, shredded
- 2 tbsp. olive oil
- 1 c. pepperoni or sausage or burger
- ½ c. various veggies, if desired
- ¾ c. pizza sauce or spaghetti sauce

- Lightly oil Dutch oven.
- Press dough into Dutch.
- Spread sauce evenly across dough.
- Place half of the pepperoni over the sauce.
- Spread cheese evenly.
- Place other half of pepperoni on top of cheese.

- Place lid on Dutch with 18–20 coals on top, 10–12 on the bottom.
- Cook for 30 minutes. Rotate lid and oven one-quarter turn every 15 minutes without lifting lid.

Steak Pizza

- o 2 tbsp. olive oil
- o 1 tsp. salt
- o 1 tbsp. Worcestershire
- o ½ lb. round steak
- o ½ an onion
- o ½ a green pepper
- o ½ batch TORYWEK
- o ¾ c. BBQ sauce (p. 177)
- o 3 c. mozzarella or jack cheese, shredded

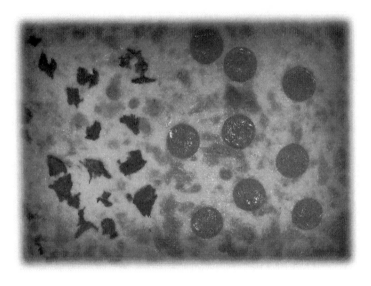

- Lightly oil Dutch and place on 24–26 coals.
- Sauté onion, pepper, and steak with 1 tsp. salt and Worcestershire for 8 minutes.
- Remove and set aside.
- Remove Dutch from heat. Let it cool slightly, and wipe it out.
- Press dough into Dutch.
- Spread sauce evenly across dough.
- Spread cheese evenly.
- Place steak and veggie mix evenly on top of cheese.
- Place lid on Dutch with 18–20 coals on top, 10–12 on the bottom.
- Cook for 30 minutes. Rotate lid and oven one-quarter turn every 15 minutes without lifting lid.

Cornbread

- 2 c. corn meal
- 3 tsp. baking powder
- 3 c. baking mix (p. 89)
- 3 eggs
- ½ c. sugar
- 2 tsp. salt
- 2 c. canned milk (or 2 c. buttermilk)

- Mix all ingredients and pour into a well-oiled Dutch.
- Place lid on Dutch, 16–18 coals on top, 10–12 on the bottom.
- Cook for 30–35 minutes. Rotate lid and oven one-quarter turn every 15 minutes without removing the lid.

Tasty Tidbit: The above recipe is a basic cornbread. Out camping, I really like to use boxed mixes. They taste great, and less measuring is involved. You can easily turn cornbread into a meal in a pot with just a few changes to the recipe. Here are some ideas:

- *Add 1 can of cream corn and 1 c. shredded cheddar.*
- *Add above and a can of green chiles and ½ lb. crumbled bacon.*
- *Pour mix over top of 6 c. chili and cook for 45 minutes.*
- *Pour mix over top of a BBQ beef recipe (p. 32) and cook for 45 minutes.*

Gorditas

- 2 c. masa maíz (MaSeCa)
- 2 c. water or broth, warm and bordering hot (I prefer broth.)
- 2 tbsp. lard (or veggie oil)
- 1 tsp. salt
- 1 tsp. baking powder
- Bowl of warm water (to keep your hands moist as we make gorditas)

- Mix all ingredients in a large bowl until a "Play-Doh®" consistency is reached.
- Roll into mounds the size of golf balls, then flatten in your palm to ¼"-thick patties.
- Stack the patties on waxed paper; separate the gorditas with waxed paper if you stack them high.
- Lightly oil the Dutch and place on 26–28 coals. We want the temperature about 375°F.
- Carefully place a gordita patty in the Dutch. Flip after 15 seconds, and cook for 3–4 minutes until golden brown. Then flip and cook for 3–4 minutes.
- Let the gordita rest for a minute while you get the next one going. Then, using a serrated knife, open the gordita into a pocket.
- Fill with green or red chile or with any meat, cabbage, salsa, and sour cream.
- Gorditas are tricky, so don't feel bad if you skip the "filling" and just place one on top and one on the bottom for a gordita sandwich.

Sourdough Starter

- 2 c. flour
- 1 tsp. sugar
- 1 tbsp. active dry yeast
- 2 c. warm water (110°F)

- Mix all ingredients together in a sterile (very clean) glass or crockery container with a capacity of at least 3 qts. (No metal, avoid plastic.)
- Store on the counter in a warm area covered by a dishcloth.
- Each day, add ⅓ c. warm water and ⅓ c. flour, then mix.
- On the seventh day, your starter will be ready to use. Rather than feeding it, it should feed you.
- Make a batch of sourdough pancakes (p. 107). (Yes, this is required; you will use up about 2 c. of your mix.)
- Repeat the feeding process for another week, then another.

Feeding the starter and eating the starter will help you produce an excellent sourdough. You can continue the process pretty much indefinitely. However, I find that after about four weeks, it is time to put the starter to rest in the fridge. Cover with plastic wrap and put a rubber band around the rim. This allows gas to escape as needed while keeping out other nasty flavors and stuff.

When you are ready to use your starter again, pull it out of the fridge. Mix the starter lightly (it will separate) and let it sit a day. Then feed it and let it sit a day, and then use it.

Pumpkin Bread

- 1 29-oz. can pumpkin puree
- 4 eggs
- 1 c. vegetable oil
- ¾ c. water
- 3 c. white sugar
- 3½ c. flour
- 2 tsp. baking soda
- 1½ tsp. salt
- 2 tbsp. ground cinnamon
- 1 tbsp. ground nutmeg
- 1 tsp. ground cloves
- 1 tbsp. ground ginger
- 2 c. chocolate chips

• Mix all wet ingredients and the sugar well, then add the spices, salt, soda, flour, and chips last.

• Pour batter into a well-oiled 14" Dutch.

• Cook with 12 coals on bottom and 18 coals on top for 55 minutes.

• You can half the recipe and use four aluminum loaf pans inside your Dutch to cook smaller loaves.

This recipe is excellent for "neighbor gifts." Use half-sized loaf pans filled with 2 c. batter. Cook in a conventional oven at 350°F for 55 minutes.

8 Breakfast

This one time at Dutch-oven camp, everyone slept in, which is quite an abnormal feat. It was already 8:30 in the morning by the time we poked our heads out of our tents, and the snow dusted us with just a couple inches. The temperature had dropped, and to say it was cold would be an "udder" statement. The water in the pot from the previous night's cocoa experience had frozen, so a roaring fire was our priority.

The warmth of the flames soon melted the ice, and steam rose from the fine little kettle. We fired up the burner and got our coals going as one of the young men began mixing eggs in a ziplock bag.

Mixing your eggs in a ziplock is a super-easy shortcut on a campout to make "personal" omelets for all. With the eggs mixed, pour a bit in the bottom of your Dutch, and then let someone "personalize it" by adding a few ingredients from other ziplocks. Cheese, peppers, mushrooms, ham, and bacon can all be made ahead of time and stored for "personalized" omelets.

Anyhoo, this particular young man had a pretty serious case of "hand and mouth" disease. If his mouth was moving, so were his hands. If you were to handcuff this individual, he would be mute. He mixed and talked and talked and mixed, and at several points, he set the bag down to make his general point with large gestures. His story finally found its crescendo, and his arms flew up, bag in tow, and then down, where the centrifugal force continued on the bag as his arms stopped.

The baggie hit the ground, and eggs splattered everywhere. I swear I could see a smiley face form in the snow. His face sank, and we all jeered and roused, but in the end, we had hash-brown sandwiches, and they weren't all that bad.

Quiche

- 2 uncooked pie crusts for a 9" pie
- 1 lb. bacon, chopped
- 1 large onion, sliced and chopped
- 1 large bell pepper, sliced and chopped
- 10 eggs
- 1 c. heavy cream
- 1 tsp. salt
- 1 tsp. pepper
- 1 tsp. mustard powder
- 2 c. sharp cheddar cheese

- Place Dutch on 24–26 coals and cook bacon just shy of crispy.
- Remove bacon and set aside.
- Add onion and bell pepper to bacon drippings; cook until soft.
- Remove onion/bell pepper mix; set aside.
- Remove Dutch from heat. Allow it to cool slightly; wipe out excess grease with paper towels.
- Get creative, and piece the pie crusts together on the bottom and 2–3" up the sides of a 12" Dutch oven liner. Place one crust on the bottom, and slice the other crust into 3" strips to form the sides.
- Mix the eggs, spices, and cream to a froth.
- Pour mixture into the crust in the Dutch liner.
- Cut bacon into pieces and sprinkle into the mix.
- Sprinkle in the onion and bell pepper.
- Add cheese evenly.

- Place liner in center of 14" Dutch.

- Place lid on oven with 16–18 coals on top, 12–14 on the bottom

- Cook for 45–50 minutes. Rotate lid and pot one-quarter turn every 15–20 minutes without removing the lid.

- Check your quiche at 30 minutes; you will probably need new coals to finish the last 10–15 minutes.

Did you know that Dutch-oven liners come in several sizes and are disposable? You can purchase them online or at most camping stores where Dutch ovens are sold. I like to keep four or five on hand at any given time. They work great for serving while the Dutch is put back to work making the next course.

Breakfast Casserole

- 1 lb. bacon, chopped
- 1 large onion, sliced and chopped
- 1 large bell pepper, sliced and chopped
- 8 c. hash-brown potatoes (fresh or frozen, uncooked)
- 2 tsp. salt
- 1 tsp. pepper
- 1 tsp. garlic powder
- 8 eggs
- 1 c. canned milk
- 2 c. sharp cheddar cheese

- Place Dutch on 24–26 coals; cook bacon just shy of crispy.
- Remove bacon and set aside.
- Add onion and bell pepper to bacon drippings; cook until soft.
- Remove onion/bell pepper mix and set aside.
- Remove Dutch from heat; allow to cool slightly and remove about half of the grease.

- Press hash browns into the bottom of the Dutch; season with half of the salt, pepper, and garlic powder.
- Place lid on the oven with 16–18 coals on top, 12–14 on the bottom.

- Cook for 30 minutes. Rotate lid and pot one-quarter turn after 15 minutes without removing the lid.

- Combine eggs, remaining spices, milk, bacon, and veggies.

- Pour mixture over the hash browns in the Dutch.

- Place lid on the oven with 16–18 coals on top, 12–14 on the bottom.

- Cook for 30 minutes. Rotate lid and pot one-quarter turn after 15 minutes without removing the lid.

Did you know that a breakfast casserole and Dutch oven full of biscuits will easily feed 12–14 people? As an added bonus, you can precut and measure all ingredients and store them in baggies, and breakfast can be ready in about an hour.

Potato Pancakes

- 4 c. mashed potatoes
- 4 eggs
- 4 tbsp. baking mix (p. 89)
- ½ lb. sausage, chopped and cooked
- ¼ c. canned milk
- 2 tsp. salt
- 1 tsp. pepper
- 1 tsp. garlic powder
- 1 c. cheese, shredded (Pick your favorite.)

- Cook sausage in the Dutch on top of 24–26 coals.
- Remove the sausage and allow to cool slightly.
- Mix all ingredients.
- Place Dutch lid upside down on 26–28 coals.
- Use paper towels to clean out sausage grease from Dutch.
- Use a grease-soaked paper towel to grease the lid.
- Scoop ½- to ¾-cup servings into the Dutch and onto the Dutch lid.
- Cook as you would a pancake, 4–5 minutes per side.
- Serve with syrup or sausage gravy. (Trust me, use the gravy, p. 185.)

Bacon Cinnamon Rolls (Omit the bacon if you're a fearful type.)

- o 1 batch TORYWEK" (p. 81)
- o 1 stick butter, softened
- o 1 c. brown sugar, packed
- o ½ c. granulated sugar
- o 1 c. bacon crumbles (Fresh is best.)
- o 2 tbsp. cinnamon
- o 1 tsp. nutmeg

- Roll out dough on a flat surface to ½" thick and about 24" x 24".
- Smear entire surface evenly with butter.
- Mix sugars and spices together; sprinkle evenly over dough.
- Sprinkle bacon crumbles on sugar.
- Roll tightly and cut into 2"-thick rolls.
- Place rolls evenly together in a well-oiled 14" Dutch.
- Place lid on Dutch with 16–18 coals on top and 10–12 on the bottom.
- Cook for 40 minutes. Rotate pot and lid every 15 minutes without removing the lid.
- Top with a maple glaze (p. 184) or cream-cheese frosting (p. 184) and serve.

Ham and Cheese Pancakes

- 2 c. baking mix (p. 89)
- 2 eggs
- 1 tbsp. vanilla extract
- ½ lb. ham, cooked and chopped
- 1 c. cheddar cheese, shredded
- 2 c. canned milk

- Combine baking mix, eggs, vanilla, and milk. (Add more milk for a thinner batter.)
- Place the Dutch on 22–24 coals.
- Oil both the lid and the Dutch oven.
- Scoop ½- to ¾-cup servings into the Dutch and onto the Dutch lid.
- Sprinkle ham and cheese onto raw batter before flipping.
- Cook as you would a pancake, 4–5 minutes per side.
- Serve with butter and a dab of fruit preserves!
- Tip: Use the lid to cook the pancakes and store them in the Dutch with only 4 coals at the outer edges to keep the cakes warm. Cover with foil until you have accumulated an army of cakes so the family can eat together.

Heavenly Pancakes

- 2 c. baking mix (p. 89)
- 2 eggs
- 1 tbsp. vanilla extract
- 2 c buttermilk
- 1 tsp. baking soda

- Combine baking mix, soda, eggs, vanilla, and milk. (Add more milk for a thinner batter.)
- Place Dutch on 22–24 coals.
- Oil both the lid and the Dutch oven.
- Scoop ½- to ¾-cup servings into the Dutch and onto the Dutch lid.
- Cook for 4–5 minutes per side.
- Serve hot off the Dutch!

Did you know that you can personalize your pancakes? Bring small containers of fillings and toppings to add to the pancakes for a little something extra. Drop some dried blueberries, candied almonds, granola, chocolate chips, or butterscotch chips into the pancake as it cooks to make it fun and tasty. Bananas or apples and caramel make great toppings too!

Sourdough Pancakes

- 2 c. sourdough starter (p. 95)
- 2 tbsp. sugar
- 2 eggs
- 4 tbsp. vegetable oil
- ½ tsp. salt
- 1 tsp. baking soda
- 1 tbsp. warm water

- Mix starter, oil, sugar, eggs, and salt together.
- Dissolve soda in warm water.
- Place Dutch on 22–24 coals.
- Oil both the lid and the Dutch oven.
- Mix soda and water mixture to the batter; let sit for 2 minutes.
- Scoop ½- to ¾-cup servings into the Dutch and onto the Dutch lid.
- Cook as you would a pancake, 4–5 minutes per side.
- Serve with honey butter!
- Use the lid to cook the pancakes and store them in the Dutch with only 4 coals at the outer edges to keep the cakes warm. Cover with foil until you have assembled a host of cakes, and then run and hide with them all for yourself!

German Pancake

- 1 c. milk
- 6 eggs
- 1 c. flour
- 1 tbsp. vanilla extract
- ½ tsp. salt
- 4 tbsp. butter
- 3 tbsp. powdered sugar

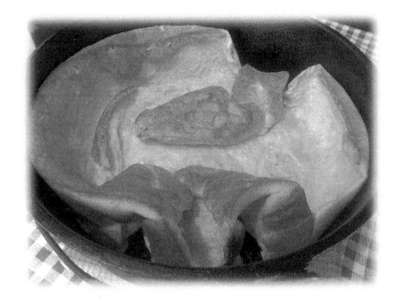

- Mix milk, eggs, flour, and salt.
- With the Dutch oven on 22–24 coals, melt the butter.
- Add mixture to Dutch.
- Place lid on the oven with 16–18 coals on top, 10–12 on the bottom.
- Cook for 40 minutes. Rotate lid and pot one-quarter turn every 10–15 minutes without removing the lid.
- Serve with butter and warm vanilla cinnamon syrup (p. 183) or maple glaze (p. 184).

French Toast (Bread Pudding Style)

- 6 tbsp. butter, melted
- 1 c. brown sugar
- 10–12 thick slices of French bread or Texas toast
- 8 eggs, beaten
- 1 c. canned milk, or whole milk
- 2 tbsp. vanilla extract
- 1 tbsp. cinnamon
- ½ tsp. nutmeg
- ½ tsp. ground ginger
- ¼ tsp. salt
- ½ c. nuts, chopped, or dried fruit if desired (pecans, almonds, raisins, blueberries)

- Mix butter and brown sugar; pour into bottom of Dutch oven. (This is a good time to use a liner for easy cleanup. You can prepare ahead of time and refrigerate for up to 12 hours.)
- Layer bread slices evenly on top of sugar mix in Dutch.
- Mix eggs, milk, vanilla, cinnamon, nutmeg, ginger, and salt; pour over bread slices. Get 'em all.
- Add chopped nuts 'n fruit, if desired.
- Place lid on the oven with 16–18 coals on top, 12–14 on the bottom.

- Cook for 45–50 minutes.

- Rotate lid and pot one-quarter turn every 10–15 minutes without removing the lid.

- Serve with warm homemade syrup (p. 183).

- To make bread pudding, replace canned milk with one 14-oz. can of sweetened condensed milk.

9 Chili and Casseroles

The giant fum'd and fo'd and fi'd, and amid his stench my senses died.

I questioned why greed brought me here, to find the gold that he held dear.

I peeked from behind a giant baguette to see him moving in the kitchenette.

He pulled from the shelf a box or two, a giant bowl, and a pot for stew.

A spice he splattered dusted the air, and my nose cried out to blow some air.

But in my hiding I must settle, or find myself inside his kettle.

He mixed in circles with bare paws and licked his fingers and picked his schnoze.

Amid the mixing he added flour, then he watched it cook for what seemed an hour.

He clutched a bowl and sat for supper, next to me and my baguette cover.

Then seizing knife to slice the bread, he missed by inches my ducking head.

He gobbled up the bread and stew and my hideout shrunk, oh what to do.

One more piece and I would be plain to see; he grabbed the bread and looked at me.

His lifeless stare my blood did thicken, and he spoke with force, "It tastes like chicken."

—Wade P. Haggard

Old Town Chili with Beans

- 3–4 lbs. ground beef (Coarsely ground is best, 93 percent lean.)
- 3 medium onions, diced
- 4 15-oz. cans pinto beans, drained and rinsed
- 4 c. beef broth
- 1 4.5-oz. can tomato paste
- 2 14-oz. cans fire-roasted, diced tomatoes
- 2 tbsp. Worcestershire
- 1 tbsp. seasoned salt
- Spices for batch number one:
  - 1 tbsp. onion powder
  - 1 tbsp. garlic powder
  - ½ tsp. Mexican oregano
  - 1 tbsp. smoked chili powder
  - 1 tbsp. chipotle chili powder
  - 1 tbsp. smoked paprika
  - 1 tbsp. beef bouillon granules
  - 1 tbsp. cumin
- Spices for batch number two:
  - 1 tbsp. cumin
  - 1 tbsp. garlic powder
  - ½ tsp. white pepper
  - ½ tsp. black pepper
  - 1 tbsp. paprika
  - 1 tbsp. chili powder

- 2 cubes caldo de tamate

- Brown beef, onion, 1 tbsp. salt, and Worcestershire in 14" Dutch on 20–22 coals.
- Add tomato paste and mix well.
- Add spice batch number one; mix while cooking for 5 minutes.
- Add tomatoes, beans, and broth.
- Add lid with 12 coals on bottom and 16 coals on top; cook for 30 minutes.
- Add spice batch number 2; mix while cooking for 5 minutes.
- Add lid, cook with 12 coals on bottom and 16 coals on top, for another 30–45 minutes.

Did you know that Mexican and Mediterranean oregano (usually labeled just "oregano") are different? Mexican oregano is a member of the lemon verbena family, while Mediterranean oregano is a member of the mint family. Mexican oregano has a citrus taste to it.

Shredded Red Beef Chili

- 3–4 lbs. chuck roast
- 2 tbsp. vegetable oil
- 1 large can red enchilada sauce, 28 oz.
- 1 medium onion, chopped
- 1 tsp. cumin
- 1 tsp. black pepper
- 1 tsp. smoked paprika
- 2 tsp. seasoned salt
- Juice of 2 limes

- Salt and pepper the chuck roast.
- With Dutch on 20–22 coals, add oil and brown both sides of roast.
- Add remaining ingredients on top of roast in the Dutch.
- Place lid on oven with 12–14 coals on top, 10–12 coals on bottom.
- Cook for 3 hours. Rotate lid and pot one-quarter turn every 15–20 minutes without removing the lid.
- Shred roast into juices; use two forks to rip meat into shreds.
- Serve with tortillas and/or rice
- Makes a great filler for enchilada casserole (p. 119).

Chili sin Frijoles (Chili without Beans)

- 4 lbs. coarse ground lean beef (93 percent lean)
- 1 package onion soup mix
- 3 tbsp. Worcestershire
- 1 4.5-oz. can tomato paste
- 2 c. beef broth
- 1 tbsp. onion powder
- 1 tbsp. garlic powder
- ½ tsp. Mexican oregano
- 1 tbsp. smoked chili powder
- 1 tbsp. chipotle chili powder
- 1 tbsp. smoked paprika
- 1 tbsp. beef bouillon granules
- 1 tbsp. cumin
- 1 7-oz. can chipotle chiles in adobo

- In a 14" Dutch, on 20–22 coals, brown beef, onion soup mix, and Worcestershire.
- Mix in tomato paste and cook for 2–3 minutes; add broth and mix.
- Add remaining ingredients and mix well.
- Place lid on oven with 12–14 coals on top, 10–12 coals on bottom.
- Cook for 2 hours. Rotate lid and pot one-quarter turn every 15–20 minutes without removing the lid.

Lasagna

- 1 lb. lean beef, ground
- 1 lb. spicy Italian sausage, ground
- 1 medium onion, diced
- 2 beef bouillon cubes, crushed
- 2 tbsp. Worcestershire sauce
- 2 tbsp. Italian Rub (p. 182)
- 3 14-oz. cans Italian tomatoes, diced or crushed
- 1 4.5-oz. can tomato paste
- 2 lbs. precooked lasagna noodles (or oven-ready)
- 16 oz. mozzarella, shredded
- 8 oz. Parmesan, shredded

- In a 14" Dutch on 22–24 coals, brown beef and sausage with onion, bouillon, and Worcestershire.
- Add tomato paste, Italian Rub, and tomatoes.
- Mix well, cooking for 5 minutes at a simmer.
- Remove meat mix from the Dutch; no need to wipe out the Dutch.
- Spread a single layer of noodles, breaking them up as necessary to fit across the bottom of the Dutch.
- Use noodles to create a "side" around the bottom of the Dutch (so you have a noodle pie crust).
- Place about one-third of the meat-sauce mixture over noodles (about 1" thick).
- Place about one-third of the cheeses on top of the meat mix.
- Add another layer of noodles; repeat the meat-sauce and cheese layers, then again.
- Place lid on the oven with 14–16 coals on top, 12–14 coals on bottom.
- Cook for 45 minutes. Rotate lid and pot one-quarter turn every 15–20 minutes without removing the lid.

Did you know that you can make the lasagna recipe at home, place it in a liner, cover it, and freeze it? Then throw the lasagna in the cooler, thaw it, and use it on the second or third day at camp for a quick meal! You can use other recipes this way as well.

Enchilada Casserole

- 4 large chicken breasts
- 1 lb. uncooked sausage (spicy or sage)
- 1 tsp. seasoned salt
- 1 tsp. black pepper
- 1 tbsp. Worcestershire
- 1 tsp. cumin
- 1 tsp. Mexican oregano
- 2 medium onions, chopped
- 2 large cans green enchilada sauce, 28 oz.
- 2 small cans diced green chiles, 4 oz.
- 2 tbsp. oil
- 1 lime (juice and zest)
- 2 lbs. shredded cheddar
- Large bag or 2 medium bags of tortilla chips

- Add oil to a 14" Dutch oven on top of 22–24 coals.
- Brown sausage in oil, creating crumbles; remove from Dutch and set aside.
- Chop chicken breast into 2" cubes.
- Brown chicken with salt, pepper, cumin, and Worcestershire, 5–8 minutes.
- Add oregano and sausage.
- Add onion, lime juice, lime zest, and green chiles; simmer for 5 minutes.
- Remove the meat from Dutch; remove Dutch from heat.
- Time to create layers; no need to wipe out the Dutch.

- Pour half a can of enchilada sauce number one into the Dutch and spread evenly.

- Create a layer of tortilla chips, about half a bag.

- Add half of your meat mix on top of chips.

- Add half of the cheese and spread evenly.

- Cover with the other half can of enchilada sauce number one.

- Create a new layer using the remaining half of chips, then meat, and then cheese.

- Pour the remaining can number two of the sauce over the top evenly.

- Place lid on the oven with 14–16 coals on top, 12–14 coals on bottom.

- Cook for 30–40 minutes. Rotate lid and pot one-quarter turn every 15 minutes without removing the lid.

Chili and Cornbread

- ½ batch chili (p. 113) or 4 cans of your favorite
- ½ batch cornbread (p. 93) or your favorite mix
- 1 can whole-kernel corn, drained
- 1 small can (4 oz.) diced green chiles, (optional)
- 1 8-oz. bag shredded cheddar cheese

- Pour chili into 14" Dutch.
- Mix remaining ingredients together; dab evenly over top of chili.
- Place lid on oven with 16–18 coals on top, 12–14 coals on bottom.
- Cook for 45 minutes to 1 hour. Rotate lid and pot one-quarter turn every 15–20 minutes without removing the lid.
- Serve with sour cream, shredded cheese, and salsa.

Taco Casserole

- 1 lb. ground beef
- 1 lb. chorizo
- 1 tbsp. The Rub (p. 181)
- 1 tsp. garlic powder
- 1 tsp. seasoned salt
- 1 medium onion
- 1 14-oz. can whole-kernel corn, drained
- 1 4-oz. can diced green chiles
- 1 16-oz. bag cheddar jack cheese, shredded
- 1 dozen precooked flour tortillas (burrito size)

- In a 14" Dutch, warm oil on 20–22 coals; brown beef and chorizo with onion and spices.
- Add corn and chiles; mix until warm. Remove meat mix from Dutch; no need to wipe it out.
- Place a layer of tortillas evenly on the bottom of the Dutch (about 4).
- Add half of the mix to the top of tortillas; sprinkle with one-third of the cheese mix.
- Create another layer of 4 tortillas, remaining meat mix and one-third of the cheese.
- Add remaining 4 tortillas in a top layer; sprinkle with remaining cheese.
- Place lid on oven with 14–16 coals on top, 12–14 coals on bottom.
- Cook for 30–45 minutes. Rotate lid and pot one-quarter turn every 15–20 minutes without removing the lid.
- Serve with sour cream, shredded cheese, and salsa.

Spicy Sausage and Potato Stew

- 2 lbs. ground pork sausage (your favorite savory flavor)
- 2 tbsp. olive oil
- 1 large onion, chopped fine
- 2 bay leaves
- ½ tsp. garlic powder
- 1 tsp. peppercorns
- ½ tsp. rosemary
- 1 tsp. crushed red pepper
- 2 tbsp. Worcestershire
- 1 package beefy onion soup mix (dry)
- 2½ lbs. red potatoes (8–10), cut into bite-size cubes
- 2 qts. beef stock
- 2 14-oz. cans milk
- ½ c. flour
- Salt to taste

- In your Dutch oven on top of 20–22 coals, add olive oil, onion, and sausage.
- Chop sausage to separate into bite-size "crumbles."
- In an herb grinder, grind peppercorns, red pepper, rosemary, and bay leaves to dust. (If you don't have an herb grinder, mince them as finely as possible; use ground pepper.)
- Add all spices, Worcestershire, and beefy onion soup mix; mix together.
- Cook sausage to just shy of brown.
- Add potatoes; cook for 5 minutes or until sausage is completely done.

- Add beef stock.

- Cook for 30 minutes at a light simmer, with 18–20 coals on bottom and 14–16 coals on top. Crack the lid at 15 minutes to allow the broth to reduce.

- Mix milk and flour completely to form a slurry.

- Remove Dutch lid and taste the broth. Now is the time to alter the flavor. More salt? More pepper? More spice?

- Add the milk/flour slurry and mix well; stir and bring to a simmer.

- Replace lid and cook another 20–30 minutes at a simmer.

- Replace the coals 18–20 on bottom and 14–16 on top.

Old-Fashioned Stew

- 3–4 lbs. stew meat
- 2 tbsp. The Rub (p. 181)
- 1 tbsp. Worcestershire
- 2 medium onions, chopped coarsely to 1"
- 6 small potatoes, chopped coarsely to 1"
- 3 large carrots, chopped coarsely to 1"
- 3 celery stalks, chopped coarsely to 1"
- 2 bay leaves
- 1 tbsp. seasoned salt
- 2 cans beef broth, about 1 qt.
- 4 tbsp. flour
- 1 tbsp. vegetable oil

* In a 14" Dutch, bring oil to temperature, about 350°, on 22–24 coals; brown beef with onion, Worcestershire, and spices.
* Add all veggies; continue browning for 5 minutes.
* Mix broth and flour together until well blended; add to Dutch.
* Place lid on oven with 14–16 coals on top, 12–14 coals on bottom.
* Cook for 1 hour and 30–45 minutes. Rotate lid and pot one-quarter turn every 15–20 minutes without removing the lid.

Tasty Tidbit: You can add biscuits to the top of your stew the last 20 minutes of cooking for stew and dumplings. Works well with any stew or soup, even chili!

Shepherd's Pie

- 3 lbs. ground beef
- 1 beef bouillon cube, crushed
- 2 tbsp. Worcestershire
- 1 large onion, sliced
- 8 potatoes, sliced thin or shredded like hash browns (If you use mashed potatoes, cut the cooking time in half.)
- 2 c. frozen veggies (peas, corn, green beans, or broccoli—you get the idea)
- 1 tsp. thyme leaves, crushed
- 1 tsp. black pepper
- 2 tbsp. flour
- 2 c. beef broth
- 1 tbsp. seasoned salt
- 2 c. cheese, shredded

- In a 14" Dutch on top of 22–24 coals, add oil; heat.
- Add beef, bouillon, Worcestershire, and onion; brown for 5–7 minutes.
- Add veggies, pepper, and thyme; mix well.
- Mix broth and flour to a slurry; mix with beef.
- Add potatoes layered to the top of beef mix; sprinkle with salt and cheese.
- Place lid on the oven with 16–18 coals on top, 12–14 coals on bottom.
- Cook for 1 hour and 30 minutes. Rotate lid and pot one-quarter turn every 15–20 minutes without removing the lid.

10 Fish and Game

Many years ago, my father and I sat in a small boat at the bottom of a dam, fishing and chatting. Just underneath the water, not more than five feet from the edge of our little boat, swam two salmon. A third approached and jumped up a swim ladder to the top of the dam.

To our disbelief, we heard a gurgled expression of amazement as one salmon exclaimed to the other, "Nice form!"

My father and I looked at one another, and we both shook our heads, knowing this was not possible and that maybe we had been in the sun too long. Perhaps it was time to reel in and find our way to the shade for an afternoon nap. But without conversation, our man pride kicked in, and we returned to fishing. A moment later, a bass swam next to the salmon, and at full speed, blasted himself head first into the bottom step of the ladder.

The first salmon, being polite, exclaimed, "No, no, no, you have to jump!"

Again, my father and I looked at one another in amazement, this time sure of what we had heard. Not wanting to scare the fish, and in a state of shock, my father and I remained silent as the bass circled our boat, building a huge wake. Again, at full speed, the bass rammed the bottom step to the swim ladder.

Once more, the salmon pleaded with the bass, "You don't understand! You have to jump at the last possible moment!" Aggravation was obvious in the salmon's tone, even through the muffled gurgles of the underwater conversation. "For the love of all that is aquatic, learn to jump." The two salmon swam a circle in frustration, jumping slightly in instruction, and regarded the other.

The bass shook himself violently, as if to awaken from a deep sleep, or in this case a concussion. Without hesitation, the bass swam backward from the step and then forward around the boat, throwing a wake large enough to tip us slightly and push us both off balance. With full force and maximum speed, the bass swam faster and faster directly toward the ladder.

I'm in Dutch!

The salmon screamed in horror, begging, "Jump! Jump! *Jump!*"

To no avail, the bass swam head first into the cement stair, knocking himself dead.

The two salmon, looking at one another, watched as the bass floated to the surface and drifted to our boat. My father reached down, grabbed the lifeless fish, and placed him in our keeper basket.

As the two salmon considered one another and the events that had unfolded, they began to swim away. Small bubbles emerged at the surface, and I swear I heard the phrase "dumb bass."

Did you know that you can place your fired coals so that they touch unfired coals to prolong the cooking time of your heat? The Dutch shown here will cook for about 90 minutes without needing more coals.

Salmon (Fillet)

While wild caught salmon is a favorite, this recipe will work for most any "fatty" fish fillet, either wild or farm-raised. Wild-caught fish have more of a "fishy" taste and smell.

- 3 lbs. of fillets, cut to cover the bottom of a 14" Dutch oven
- 2 tbsp. fresh dill
- 1 tsp. pepper
- 1 lemon, zested and juiced
- 1½ tsp. seasoned salt

- Begin by placing the fillets on parchment paper in the shape and size of the bottom of your Dutch.
- Mix all herbs, zest, and spices.
- Smear the herb mixture evenly over fillets.
- Pick up fillets on parchment and drop them into the Dutch oven.
- Place lid on the oven with 16–18 coals on top, 12–14 coals on bottom.
- Cook for 30 minutes. Rotate lid and pot one-quarter turn every 15–20 minutes without removing the lid.
- For an all-in-one-pot meal, coat fresh asparagus spears with olive oil, salt, and pepper. Place the asparagus atop the salmon before cooking.

Trout (Whole)

- 4–6 whole trout (12"), gutted and cleaned
- 2 lemons, zested and juiced
- 2 tbsp. olive oil
- ½ c. Dijon mustard
- 1 garlic clove, crushed and minced
- 1 tbsp. seasoned salt
- 1 tsp. white pepper
- Pinch of crushed red pepper

- Mix oil, Dijon, lemon zest, lemon juice, and red pepper together.
- Season trout with salt and pepper.
- Spread Dijon mix evenly all over inside and outside of each trout.
- Place trout on top of parchment paper in Dutch.
- Place lid on the oven with 14–16 coals on top, 12–14 coals on bottom.
- Cook for 25–30 minutes. Rotate lid and pot one-quarter turn every 15–20 minutes without removing the lid.

Halibut (Fish 'n Chips)

- 3 lbs. halibut (or other firm fish), cut evenly into fingerling strips
- 2 c. flour
- ½ c. cornstarch
- 1 tbsp. baking powder
- 16 oz. dark beer (If no beer, use half water and half buttermilk.)
- 2 tbsp. lemon pepper
- 2 tbsp. Italian Rub (p. 182)
- Dusting of flour for halibut (about 2 tbsp.)
- 1 qt. or so of vegetable or peanut oil

- Pat halibut strips dry; season with lemon pepper.
- Dust halibut lightly with 2 tbsp. of flour.
- Prepare Dutch oven on 28–30 coals on bottom (To deep-fry at 350°F, you will need to cover the bottom in coals.)
- Pour in about 2–3" of vegetable oil.
- Mix flour, cornstarch, Italian Rub, baking powder, and beer into a batter.
- Dip strips into batter; fry for 5–7 minutes or until golden brown and the fish are flaky.
- Serve with fries or chips (p. 143) and coleslaw (p. 146).

Wild Red Meat Steak

- 3–4 lbs. 1"-thick wild red meat steaks (elk, deer, bison, antelope), with any silver skin removed
- 3 tbsp. rice vinegar
- 3 tbsp. lime juice
- 3 tbsp. Worcestershire
- 3 tbsp. honey
- ¼ c. The Rub (p. 181)
- 1 tbsp. seasoned salt
- 2 tbsp. peanut oil

- Season steaks with The Rub.
- Mix vinegar, Worcestershire, lime juice, and honey into a marinade.
- Place steaks in a ziplock bag and pour in marinade; refrigerate overnight.
- Remove steaks from refrigerator 30 minutes before cooking.
- Place 14" Dutch on 20 coals; preheat peanut oil.
- Just before cooking, season steaks with salt.
- Cook one or two steaks at a time in the Dutch, 5–6 minutes per side (or to desired doneness)
- Goes great with Italian Roast Potatoes (p. 140) or baked potatoes (p. 141).

Wild Red Meat Roast

- 3–4 lbs. wild red meat roast (elk, deer, bison, antelope), with any silver skin removed
- 3 tbsp. The Rub (p. 181)
- 1 tbsp. ginger
- 1 tbsp. paprika
- 5 large carrots, chopped coarsely
- 5 large parsnips, chopped coarsely
- 3 large turnips, chopped coarsely
- 2 medium onions, chopped coarsely
- 1 c. beef broth
- ½ c. apple juice
- 1 tbsp. seasoned salt
- 1 tsp. ground pepper

- Rub the roast with The Rub, ginger, and paprika.
- Season the vegetables with olive oil, salt, and pepper.
- Place veggies in a 14" Dutch with the roast on top.
- Pour broth and juice into Dutch over the veggies.
- Place lid on the oven with 14–16 coals on top, 12–14 coals on bottom.
- Cook for 1 hour and 30 minutes. Rotate lid and pot one-quarter turn every 15–20 minutes without removing the lid.

Venison or Elk Bacon Burger

- o 3 lbs. ground elk or venison (No added suet; you can also do this with lean beef.)
- o ½ lb. raw bacon, finely chopped (It helps to chop it while it's slightly frozen.)
- o 2 tbsp. beef bouillon granules
- o 1 small onion, chopped fine
- o 2 tbsp. Worcestershire sauce

- Dissolve granules in Worcestershire.
- In a 14" Dutch with 20 coals underneath, cook bacon to "near done"; remove bacon from Dutch.
- Mix all ingredients together well.
- Scoop ½ c. of meat into your hand, then press into 1" burger patties.
- In a 14" Dutch with 20 coals underneath, grill burgers for 6 minutes per side or until desired doneness.
- Serve on freshly made TORYWEK Rolls (p. 81) with lettuce, tomato, and a jalapeño pickle.*

Wait...you have never had a jalapeño pickle? Run to the store now, and purchase equal-size jars of hot jalapeño slices and bread and butter pickle slices. Now, sporting your favorite lab coat, rubber gloves, and goggles, switch the fruits of one jar to the other, or conversely, the juice, but not both. Let the mixtures sit refrigerated for a week before trying your newly found guilty pleasure: jalapeño pickles or pickled jalapeños.

Elk Roast in Bacon

- 3–4 lbs. elk roast
- 1 lb. peppered bacon
- 3 tbsp. Mexican Rub (p. 180)
- 2 tbsp. lime juice
- 8 medium potatoes, quartered
- 2 tbsp. seasoned salt

- Rub the roast with lime juice, then season with Mexican Rub.
- Cover roast in bacon. Get creative, and cover the entire roast, top and bottom.
- Season potatoes with salt.
- In a well-oiled 14" Dutch, rest the roast in the center.
- Surround roast with seasoned potatoes.
- Place lid on the oven with 14–16 coals on top, 12–14 coals on bottom.
- Cook for 1 hour and 30 minutes. Rotate lid and pot one-quarter turn every 15–20 minutes without removing the lid.

Did you know that wild-game meats are far leaner than domestic cuts? Be careful with cooking times, and don't be afraid to introduce a little fat to the cooking party.

11 Side Dishes

Who is Abbot without Costello?

Or the Hall without the Oates?

How about Chewie along Han Solo?

And Tenacious D's shimmering notes?

Where would Penn be without his Teller?

And who would pull Kermit's strings?

Who would be Ernie's favorite feller,

if Bert wouldn't help him sing?

My friends, a scoop of importance,

in all the pairs we list.

The sidekick adds the flavor,

to the final partnership.

—Wade P. Haggard

Cheesy Potatoes

- 8 medium potatoes (Yukons work great, but whatever you have will do.)
- 3 tbsp. Italian Rub (p. 182)
- 2 tsp. seasoned salt
- 1 c. sour cream
- 1 c. cream cheese, at room temperature
- 2 c. cheddar (or your favorite cheese), shredded
- 2 medium onions, sliced and diced (Using ¼ cup of bacon crumbles is also acceptable.)

• Cut potatoes into 2" cubes (You can peel them if you want; I like them rough.)

• Mix onion and potatoes in a bowl.

• Mix sour cream into cream cheese and then into shredded cheese.

• Sprinkle spices over potatoes.

• Combine remaining ingredients and mix well.

• Pour all ingredients into a 14" Dutch oven (I recommend using a greased liner.)

• Place lid on the oven with 16–18 coals on top, 12–14 coals on bottom.

• Cook for 1 hour and 20 minutes. Rotate lid and pot one-quarter turn every 15–20 minutes without removing the lid.

Did you know that this Cheesy Potato recipe is occasionally called "funeral potatoes"? I will be a little miffed if you wait until my funeral to make me some. You can add some cubed ham; crumbled, cooked sausage; or chopped cooked bacon to the potatoes before cooking to make Cheesy Potatoes a one-pot dinner. You also can precook and freeze the dinner and take it to camp for a quick "warmup."

Italian Roasted Potatoes

- o 8 medium red potatoes
- o 3 tbsp. Italian Rub (p. 182)
- o 1 tsp. seasoned salt
- o ⅓ c. olive oil
- o 2 medium onions, sliced and diced

- Cut potatoes into 2" cubes (You can peel them if you want; I like them rough.)
- Mix onion and potatoes in a bowl with olive oil.
- Sprinkle spices and salt over potatoes; combine well.
- Pour all ingredients into a 14" Dutch oven.
- Place lid on the oven with 16–18 coals on top, 12–14 coals on bottom.
- Cook for 1 hour. Rotate lid and pot one-quarter turn every 15–20 minutes without removing the lid.

Baked Potatoes

- 6–8 large Russet potatoes
- 2 tbsp. olive oil
- 1 tbsp. seasoned salt

* Clean the potatoes; rub them with oil and salt.
* Place potatoes in Dutch oven.
* Place lid on the oven with 16–18 coals on top, 12–14 coals on bottom.
* Cook for 1 hour and 30 minutes. Rotate lid and pot one-quarter turn every 15–20 minutes without removing the lid. (Move the Dutch so that the potatoes will shuffle around inside. This keeps the potatoes from getting overcooked on the bottom.)

Did you know that baked potatoes are the easiest recipe to use if you want to win Dutch-oven-cooking acclaim? Prepare all the fixings for a potato bar: bacon, butter, shredded cheese, salsa, sour cream, chives, onion, salt, and pepper. Whip up a batch of baked potatoes, and watch as everyone falls in love with you!

Hash Browns

- o 8 medium potatoes, any variety
- o 2 tbsp. vegetable oil
- o 1 tbsp. seasoned salt
- o 1 tsp. onion powder
- o 1 tsp. pepper
- o 2 medium onions, chopped fine

- Clean and shred the potatoes. (I like to use a sturdy cheese grater.)
- Mix potatoes and onion.
- Sprinkle potatoes and onion with oil, pepper, onion powder, and salt.
- Place potatoes and onion in Dutch oven.
- Place lid on the oven with 16–18 coals on top, 12–14 coals on bottom.
- Cook for 1 hour. Rotate lid and pot one-quarter turn every 15–20 minutes without removing the lid.

Fries or Chips

- 6–8 large potatoes (I like Russets because they make crispier fries due to a high starch content.)
- Enough oil to fill the Dutch one-third full, about 2 qts.
- 1 tbsp. seasoned salt

- Clean the potatoes.
- Slice the potatoes into fries or chips.
- Fill the Dutch one-third full of vegetable or peanut oil.
- Place Dutch oven on 26–28 coals; bring temp to 350°F to 375°F. (Use a thermometer.)
- Cook until golden brown in small batches (about 5 minutes).
- Drain on a rack over paper (not directly on paper).
- Sprinkle with salt while hot.

Did you know that it is a bad idea to cook with a Dutch oven in flip-flops? The coals tend to crackle and pop as you move them. Once, an ember bounced under my foot and melted its way into the rubber of my flip-flop. Needless to say, as I flipped and flopped to get my foot out of them, I got burned!

Fried Zucchini

- 6 smallish zucchini (6–8" long, 2–3" round)
- 1 batch beer batter (p. 90)
- 1 tbsp. seasoned salt

• Slice zucchini into quarters lengthwise and then halfwise.

• Season zucchini with salt; set aside.

• Mix dry ingredients for beer batter breading.

• Dust seasoned zucchini with 2 tbsp. of dry batter mix.

• Complete the batter by mixing in the liquid.

• Prepare a 14" Dutch on top of 30–32 coals, or use a burner to bring the oil temp to 375°F–400°F. (Use a thermometer, and keep the oil in this range.)

• Dip the zucchini into the batter; fry for 3–5 minutes.

• Drain on a rack to avoid oil puddles.

• Goes great with an Italian Beef Sandwich (p. 43) and some coleslaw (p. 146).

Did you know that a basic round glass candy thermometer is an easy and necessary Dutch-oven companion? The side spring is large enough to clip to the fat edge of your Dutch!

Hot German Potato Salad

- 8 medium red potatoes, sliced into ½" sections
- ½ lb. bacon
- 2 medium onions, chopped
- 2 tbsp. flour
- 2 tbsp. granulated sugar
- 2 tsp. salt
- ½ tsp. celery seed
- 1 c. chicken broth
- ½ c. cider vinegar
- A couple dashes of pepper

- In a 14" Dutch oven on top of 24–26 coals, cook bacon until crisp; remove bacon and set aside.
- Cook potatoes and onion in bacon fat, occasionally stirring until starting to soften, about 10 minutes.
- Mix broth, spices, vinegar, sugar, and flour well; pour over potatoes.
- Crumble the bacon and add to potatoes.
- Mix lightly so that the potatoes are well covered with the mix.
- Place lid on the oven with 16–18 coals on top, 12–14 coals on bottom.
- Cook for 1 hour and 20 minutes. Rotate lid and pot one-quarter turn every 15–20 minutes without removing the lid.

Coleslaw

- o 1 head of cabbage (red, green, or any combination), sliced thin
- o 2 medium onions, sliced thin
- o 2 large carrots, shredded
- o 4 stalks celery, sliced thin
- o 1 c. apple cider vinegar
- o 1 c. granulated sugar
- o 2 c. mayonnaise (or more to desired taste and texture)
- o 1 tbsp. dry mustard
- o 1 tsp. celery seed
- o ½ tsp. white pepper
- o 1 tsp. seasoned salt

- Mix vinegar, sugar, and spices until sugar dissolves. (It helps to heat in a small pan.)
- Refrigerate for 4 hours.
- Mix in mayonnaise.
- Mix in all the veggies with the cabbage.
- Add sauce as desired. (I prefer to add sauce like dressing rather than mixing it all together.)

Dutch Fried Rice

- 6 c. cooked rice (brown, white, or jasmine)
- ½ c. frozen peas
- ½ c. frozen corn
- 1 c. ham, cubed
- 1 medium onion, sliced thin
- 2 eggs
- ½ c. peanut oil (or vegetable)
- ½ c. oyster sauce
- 1 tbsp. fish sauce
- ½ c. soy sauce (or to taste)
- 1 6-oz. can water chestnuts, drained

- With Dutch on 22–24 coals, add peanut oil and bring to a shimmer, 350°F.
- Mix eggs together thoroughly; add a dash of soy sauce.
- Fry in hot oil until done, like a small omelet; remove and set aside.
- Add onion, corn, peas, and ham to Dutch.
- Cook for 3–5 minutes, until warm and onion is translucent.
- Add rice, soy sauce, oyster sauce, fish sauce, and water chestnuts.
- Cook and mix until warm throughout (10 minutes).
- Chop egg and add to rice; mix well.
- Add additional soy sauce as needed for flavor.

Spanish Rice

- 3 c. uncooked jasmine rice
- 3 tbsp. olive oil
- 2 cloves garlic, crushed and diced
- 5 c. chicken stock
- 1 6-oz. can tomato paste
- 1 tsp. Mexican oregano
- 1 tbsp. Mexican Rub (p. 180)
- 1 tbsp. seasoned salt
- ¼ c. frozen corn

- With Dutch oven on 22–24 coals, bring oil to about 350°F.
- Add rice; brown for 4–5 minutes.
- Add salt, oregano, corn, and garlic; cook for 2 more minutes.
- Add stock, Rub, and tomato paste; mix thoroughly.
- Place lid on oven with 16–18 coals on top, 12–14 coals on bottom.
- Cook for 30 minutes.
- Rotate lid and pot one-quarter turn every 15–20 minutes without removing the lid.
- Let stand for 15 minutes, covered and off the heat.

Lemon Rice

- o 3 c. uncooked jasmine rice
- o 3 tbsp. olive oil
- o Juice and zest of 3 lemons
- o 5 c. chicken broth
- o 2 tbsp. salt
- o 1 tsp. ground ginger

- Juice and zest the lemons.
- With Dutch oven on 22–24 coals, bring oil to about 350°F.
- Add the rice and lemon juice; cook for 4–5 minutes.
- Add salt, ginger, zest, and broth
- Place lid on oven with 16–18 coals on top, 12–14 coals on bottom.
- Cook for 30 minutes.
- Rotate lid and pot one-quarter turn every 15–20 minutes without removing the lid.

Baked Beans

- 4 c. raw beans (soaked 24 hrs. in cold water)
- 1 lb. bacon, chopped
- 2 medium onions, chopped roughly
- 3 tbsp. The Rub (p. 181)
- 1 c. Best BBQ Sauce Ever! (p. 177)
- 2 tbsp. prepared yellow mustard
- 3 c. beef broth
- 1 6-oz. can tomato paste

- To soak beans, cover them with cool tap water. Check back every few hours; refill as needed. Soak for 24 hours. Discard soaking water before cooking.
- In Dutch, over 22–24 coals, cook bacon until just shy of done.
- Add the onion; cook until translucent.
- Add all ingredients, minus the beans; mix thoroughly.
- Add beans.
- Place lid on the oven with 12–14 coals on top, 14–16 coals on bottom.
- Cook for 2 hours and 30 minutes.
- Rotate the lid and pot one-quarter turn every 15–20 minutes without removing the lid.

12 Desserts

Desserts are awesome! The best way to get Scouts in line is to mention dessert. The sticky goodness is not always fun to clean up, so when cooking dessert, I do the unthinkable—I use a liner. Not always do I commit this grave sin for which the purest of Dutcher would have me strung up and ladled, but on occasion I do. I offer no apology, but I will give you a choice; the recipes and cooking time are the same. I will also give you a warning: paper liners do not work, so I use the aluminum ones (great for storing leftovers, too). Another liner advantage is size—you can use a 12" or 10" liner to line a 14" oven. Just center it inside, thus making the dessert a smaller portion, if desired, without packing extra ovens.

This one time at Camp Dutch, the boys not doing much, at suggestion they made some ice cream.

One willing young man with bowl in his hand jumped in line and yelled, "Me first!" with a gleam.

"I thought you abstained 'cause milk causes you pain," I inquired of the eager young lad.

"It will be OK, as I brought some first aid, and with these pills it won't hurt so bad."

I scooped his bowl to the rim, the first time, then again, and it seemed that all would be fine.

He ate every bite, and we all said good night, so relaxed fine slumber was mine.

Later that night came shrill screams set to fright, from an outhouse marked clearly "In Conference."

"I'd do it again; it was WORTH in the end, and curse you, my lactose intolerance."

—Wade P. Haggard

Cobbler

Cobbler has a variety of styles. In general, when I say "Dutch-oven cobbler," I think of fruit covered in a crust, crumb, or cake—in short, "breading and fruiting." Below I give the recipes in a deconstructed fashion. "Deconstructed" means that I intend to show you how to make the breading and the fruiting so you can mix and match and make your favorite combination. The "breading" recipes give you the cooking instructions.

Cake-Style Fruit Cobbler

- 2 c. flour
- 1¼ c. sugar
- 1½ c. milk
- 1 tsp. baking powder
- ½ tsp. salt
- 2 tbsp. vegetable oil
- 2 eggs, slightly beaten
- 1 tbsp. vanilla extract
- 1 tsp. cinnamon
- ½ tsp. nutmeg

- Mix together all ingredients until smooth.
- In a 12" Dutch oven liner, pour your favorite fruit pie filling:
    - Homemade cherry filling (p. 159)
    - Peach fruit filling (p. 160)
    - Frozen berry filling (p. 161)
    - Or use 4 16-oz. cans of your favorite fruit pie filling.
- Spoon batter over fruit filling.
- Place liner in the center of the 14" Dutch oven.
- Place lid on oven with 16–18 coals on top, 12–14 coals on bottom.
- Cook for 45–55 minutes.
- Rotate lid and pot one-quarter turn every 15–20 minutes without removing the lid.
- Let stand for 15–20 minutes before serving.

Shortbread Biscuit Fruit Cobbler

- ⅔ c. granulated sugar
- 2 c. flour
- 1½ c. cold butter

- Cream butter and sugar together.
- Add flour until the mix is like clay.
- Roll or press out to ½" thick; cut into square or round 3" cookies.
- In a 12" Dutch oven liner, pour your favorite fruit pie filling:
  - Homemade cherry filling (p. 159)
  - Peach fruit filling (p. 160)
  - Frozen berry filling (p. 161)
  - Or use 4 16-oz. cans of your favorite fruit pie filling.
- Place shortbread on top of fruit mix.
- Place liner in the center of a 14" Dutch oven.
- Place lid on the oven with 16–18 coals on top, 12–14 coals on bottom.
- Cook for 25–30 minutes.
- Rotate lid and pot one-quarter turn every 15–20 minutes without removing the lid.
- Let stand for 15–20 minutes before serving.

Shortcake Fruit Cobbler

- 2 c. flour
- 4 tsp. baking powder
- 1 tsp. salt
- 2 tbsp. sugar
- 2 tbsp. butter
- 2 tbsp. shortening
- ¾ c. canned milk

- Mix all dry ingredients together.
- Mix shortening and butter into dry ingredients.
- Mix in milk.
- In a 12" Dutch oven liner, pour your favorite fruit pie filling:
  - Homemade cherry filling (p. 159)
  - Peach fruit filling (p. 160)
  - Frozen berry filling (p. 161)
  - Or use 4 16-oz. cans of your favorite fruit pie filling.
- Use a large spoon to dab the mixture over the fruit mix.
- Place a liner in the center of a 14" Dutch oven.
- Place lid on the oven with 16–18 coals on top, 12–14 coals on bottom.
- Cook for 30–35 minutes.
- Rotate lid and pot one-quarter turn every 15–20 minutes without removing the lid.
- Let stand for 15–20 minutes before serving.

Oatmeal Crumble Cobbler

- 1 c. flour
- 1 c. rolled oats
- 1 c. brown sugar
- ½ c. butter, melted
- ½ tsp. salt
- 2 tsp. cinnamon
- 1 tbsp. vanilla extract
- 8 oz. fruit juice or soda (lemon-lime or ginger ale, optional)

- Mix all ingredients, minus the juice/soda, until crumbly.
- In a 12" Dutch oven liner, pour your favorite fruit pie filling:
  - Homemade cherry filling (p. 159)
  - Peach Fruit filling (p. 160)
  - Frozen berry filling (p. 161)
  - Or use 4 16-oz. cans of your favorite fruit pie filling.
- Spread over top of fruit mixture.
- Sprinkle top with juice/soda (optional).
- Place liner in the center of a 14" Dutch oven.
- Place lid on oven with 16–18 coals on top, 12–14 coals on bottom.
- Cook for 30–35 minutes.
- Rotate lid and pot one-quarter turn every 15–20 minutes without removing the lid.
- Let stand for 15–20 minutes before serving.

This one time at Dutch-oven camp, when I was a youth, I awakened bright-eyed and bushy-tailed, bouncing from friend to friend, much the way a lap dog bounces from one guest to another. I was a morning person. We each had our breakfast of pancakes and syrup, and with my sweet tooth, I had a bit extra on the syrup side. I love syrup. I stood talking to a friend while yet another of my companions sat in a chair beneath me eating his breakfast quietly. He was not a morning person. It was a cold morning, and each of us was bundled up well. Oddly, my pancake seemed to be soaking up more syrup than normal, so naturally I kept adding extra. After 10 minutes or so, the boy sitting below my plate screamed because the syrup had finally soaked its way through his layers. You see, as I was talking, my paper plate had folded and funneled all my syrup down the back of this young man's sweater. Needless to say, he wasn't very pleased with me. Luckily, he was a sweet kid.

Fruit Filling

Can you use canned pie filling? Yes. Do I recommend it? No. For just a few moments effort, your taste buds and Dutcher reputation will be greatly rewarded. Canned goods are needed and necessary, and if you can your own, more's the better. If not, no worries; there are plenty of shortcuts that will give you great results. With that warning, any one of the breading recipes mentioned atop a few cans of pie filling yields a good cobbler. Nevertheless, let's make a *great* cobbler.

Cherry Pie Filling

- o 4 cans tart pie cherries (whole fruit, not the filling)
- o Juice from 1 can of the cherries; discard the remainder
- o 1 c. granulated sugar
- o 1 lime, juiced
- o 4 tbsp. cornstarch
- o 1 tsp. almond extract
- o 2 tbsp. butter

- Drain juice from three cans; retain the juice of one can.
- Whisk juice, almond extract, and cornstarch together until thoroughly mixed.
- Add the sugar; continue mixing until dissolved.
- Add cherries; dab the top with butter.
- Place fruit mix in a 12" Dutch oven liner; place liner in the center of a 14" Dutch.
- Choose breading type:
  - o Cake Style (p. 154)
  - o Shortbread Style (p. 155)
  - o Shortcake Style (p. 156)
  - o Oatmeal Crumble (p. 157)
- Cook according to breading instructions.

Peach Pie Filling

- 3 29-oz. cans of peaches (I prefer the "lite" version.)
- ½ c. brown sugar
- 2 tbsp. lime juice
- 1 tbsp. vanilla extract
- 2 tbsp. cornstarch
- 2 tbsp. butter

- Drain peaches; reserve ½ c. juice.
- Mix peach and lime juice with cornstarch and extract; mix thoroughly.
- Add brown sugar; mix well.
- Place fruit and juice mix into a 14" Dutch oven liner; place liner in a 14" Dutch.
- Choose breading type:
    - Cake Style (p. 154)
    - Shortbread Style (p. 155)
    - Shortcake Style (p. 156)
    - Oatmeal Crumble (p. 157)
- Cook according to breading instructions.

You can use fresh fruit in your cobbler. Guestimate the equivalent measurement, and be aware that fresh fruit is sometimes very juicy and other times very dry. You will have to account for this factor and add or remove liquid as needed.

Frozen Berry Pie Filling (most any type)

- 8 c. frozen berries
- ¼ c. cornstarch
- 1 c. granulated sugar
- ½ c. brown sugar
- ¼ c. lime juice
- 2 tbsp. butter

* Mix all ingredients together.
* Place fruit mix in a 12" Dutch oven liner; place liner in center of a 14" Dutch.
* Choose breading type:
  - Cake Style (p. 154)
  - Shortbread Style (p. 155)
  - Shortcake Style (p. 156)
  - Oatmeal Crumble (p. 157)
* Cook according to breading instructions.

Apple

Apple dessert is one of my personal favorites, and it takes some elbow grease to make it perfect. Right out of the gate, let me say that there are canned spiced apples that will do the trick—whole fruit, not filling. However, follow me for a minute to heaven.

You will need a cordless drill with a ½" to 1" wood "hole bit" (the flat drill bit with the point). You will also need a vegetable peeler. Start with a bag of your favorite apples; 12 to 14 should work. Clean the drill and bit thoroughly.

With the bit in the drill and the drill set to low speed, take the drill in one hand and an apple in the other. Press the drill bit into the core of the apple, about halfway through. Do not core the apple at this time. The drill should be off; you are just "skewering" the apple. Now, get the apple spinning on the drill, and with the veggie peeler, remove the peel quickly and easily. Once the peel is gone, stop the drill, grab the apple, and "core it" using the drill bit. Slice thin on a mandolin, and *presto*!

OK, it works, and it is fun, but you can do it the old-fashioned way if you want, with a knife and cutting board.

Did you know that you can use three premade pie crusts to make a 12" Dutch-oven pie? Use one crust on the bottom. Slice the second into 3" strips, and use them to create the side crust. Use the last crust on top of the cherry filling recipe (p. 159). With 18 coals on top and 12 on the bottom of a 14" Dutch, cook for 1 hour.

Apple Pie

- 10–12 apples, peeled, cored, and sliced thinish
- 1½ c. granulated sugar
- ¼ c. flour
- ½ tsp. salt
- 2 tsp. cinnamon
- 1 tsp. nutmeg
- ¼ c. lime juice
- 2 pie crusts (p. 90)

- Mix all dry ingredients together thoroughly.
- Add lime juice to apples.
- Mix apples (with juice) to dry ingredients.
- Press one pie crust into the bottom of a 12" Dutch oven liner.
- Brush the crust lightly with corn syrup (1 tsp.).
- Place fruit mix in a 12" Dutch-oven-liner crust.
- Cover fruit with second crust; cut two 3"-long venting slits in the center of the crust.
- Place liner in the center of a 14" Dutch.
- Place lid on the oven with 16–18 coals on top, 12–14 coals on bottom. (Raw apples may need a touch more heat on the bottom.)
- Cook for 40–45 minutes.
- Rotate lid and pot one-quarter turn every 15–20 minutes without removing the lid.
- Let stand for 15–20 minutes before serving.

Cheater Cheater Cobbler Eater (Basic Easy Cobbler)

- 6 c. favorite fruit filling
- 1 package favorite cake mix
- 1 stick of butter, 8 tbsp.
- Small can (8 oz.) of ginger ale

- Place fruit in a 12" liner; sprinkle cake mix on top.
- Chop butter into pats and spread evenly atop cake mix.
- Pour ginger ale over cake mix.
- Place liner in the center of a 14" Dutch oven.
- Place lid on oven with 16–18 coals on top, 12–14 coals on bottom.
- Cook for 45–55 minutes.
- Rotate lid and pot one-quarter turn every 15–20 minutes without removing the lid.
- Let stand for 15–20 minutes before serving.

Cakes and Brownies

Cakes and brownies are a staple of any camp, or they should be. They are easy to mix up from scratch. There are also good choices from the box. These sweet treats are a great way to get the kids involved with cooking. Boxed and scratch-baked goods also lend themselves to easy alteration for a variety of flavors and textures. Changing the quantity is as easy as adjusting the pan size. Keep in mind that you can use a smaller liner inside a larger Dutch oven. I prefer to use a liner, 12" inside of a 14" Dutch. A 12" liner has roughly the same volume (–10 percent) as two 9" rounds, making most classic recipes a "no brainer." Liners need to be well greased and floured for cakes and brownies.

I have included a couple recipes for cake from scratch; I also include one or two "boxed" alternatives for easy prep and a tasty treat. When baking in the Dutch, the majority—two-thirds—of your heat should come from above. Therefore, for a typical cake or brownie, using 20–22 coals on top, 10 on bottom, will do the trick. Read the section on temperature control (p. 18).

When rotating the Dutch and lid with cakes, be very gentle.

Chocolate Cake

The following ingredients are the equivalent of about two boxed mixes:

- 3⅓ c. flour
- 3 c. sugar
- 1⅓ c. cocoa (I like dark the best.)
- 1 c. vegetable oil
- 3 c. buttermilk
- 3 tsp. baking soda
- 2 tsp. salt
- 1 tbsp. vanilla
- 4 eggs
- 1 tsp. ground cinnamon

- Preheat your oven. Use 20 coals on top and 10 on the bottom to get your Dutch hot.
- Grease and flour a 12" liner.
- Mix all ingredients by hand until smooth, about 4 minutes.
- Pour batter into a greased and floured liner; place liner in center of Dutch oven.
- Cook 45–55 minutes (rotating the lid and the Dutch every 20 minutes) or until the edges start to pull away, or until a toothpick or knife inserted in the center of the cake pulls out clean.
- Just for kicks, add 1 tbsp. ground crushed red pepper for a chili chocolate cake.
- Half this recipe and cover it with cherry filling for a Black Forest Cobbler.

Yellow Cake

These ingredients are the equivalent of about two boxed mixes:

- 3 c. flour
- 2 c. sugar
- ¾ c. vegetable oil
- 1⅓ c. milk
- 1 tbsp. baking powder
- 1½ tsp. salt
- 2 tsp. vanilla
- 4 eggs

- Preheat your oven. Use 20 coals on top and 10 on the bottom to get your Dutch hot.
- Grease and flour a 12" liner.
- Mix all ingredients by hand until smooth, about 4 minutes.
- Pour batter in greased and floured liner; place liner in center of Dutch oven.
- Cook 45–55 minutes or until edges start to pull away or until a toothpick or knife inserted in the center of the cake pulls out clean.
- Rotate the lid and Dutch every 20 minutes.
  - For an excellent Egg Nog Cake, substitute rum extract for the vanilla and add 1 tsp. nutmeg and ½ tsp. ginger.

Brownies

- 2 c. cocoa (I like dark.)
- 2½ c. flour
- 2 c. sugar
- 1 c. butter (soft)
- 3 tsp. vanilla
- 4 eggs
- 1 tsp. baking powder
- 1 tsp. salt
- 1 c. chocolate chips (Pick your favorite; I like dark.)

- Preheat your oven. Use 20 coals on top and 10 on the bottom to get your Dutch hot.
- Grease a 12" liner.
- Mix sugar, butter, vanilla, and eggs.
- Mix in remaining ingredients.
- Pour batter into greased liner.
- Place liner in center of Dutch oven.
- Cook for 40–45 minutes or until a toothpick or knife inserted in the center of the cake pulls out clean. (Don't overcook.)
- Rotate lid and Dutch every 15 minutes.

Pineapple Upside-Down Cake

- ½ yellow cake recipe (p. 167) or 1 boxed cake mix
- 2 cans pineapple rings, drained
- 1 c. packed brown sugar
- ½ c. butter (soft)
- Several maraschino cherries

- Preheat your oven. Use 18 coals on top and 12 on the bottom to get your Dutch hot.
- Grease and flour a 12" liner.
- Arrange pineapple rings to cover bottom of liner; place cherries in centers, if desired.
- Mix sugar and butter in ziplock bag; distribute evenly over pineapple slices.
- Pour batter over pineapple arrangement in greased and floured liner; place liner in center of Dutch oven.
- Cook for 30–40 minutes or until edges start to pull away.
- Rotate lid and Dutch every 20 minutes.

Did you know, you could make a tres leches cake out of the yellow cake on p.167? Poke a few holes in your cake with the round end of a wooden spoon. Drizzle equal parts (1/4 c. each), cream, evaporated milk, and sweetened condensed milk over cake.

Pumpkin Spice Cake

- 1 boxed spice cake mix
- 1 29-oz. can spiced pumpkin puree
- 1 c. canned milk

- Preheat your oven. Use 20 coals on top and 10 on the bottom to get your Dutch hot.
- Grease and flour a 12" liner.
- Mix all ingredients by hand until smooth, about 4 minutes.
- Pour batter in greased and floured liner; place liner in center of Dutch oven.
- Cook for 30–40 minutes or until edges start to pull away or until a toothpick or knife inserted in the center of the cake pulls out clean.
- Rotate lid and Dutch every 10 minutes.

Key Lime Pie (because I can)

- Shortbread crust, premade and packaged in a tin
- ½ c. fresh lime juice (about 4 limes)
- Zest of 2 limes
- 1 14-oz. can sweetened condensed milk
- 5 egg yolks

- Preheat your oven. Use 22 coals on top and 12 on the bottom to get your Dutch hot.
- Mix lime juice, eggs, lime zest, and condensed milk until smooth.
- Pour into premade shell.
- Place in center of Dutch oven.
- Cook 15 minutes or until set.
- Cool completely and serve.

Pumpkin Spice Donuts

- 3 c. flour
- ½ c. pumpkin, canned
- 2 tsp. baking powder
- 1 tsp. salt
- 1 tsp. nutmeg
- 1 tbsp. pumpkin pie spice
- ½ c. sugar
- 2 tbsp. butter-flavored shortening
- 2 eggs
- 1 tbsp. vanilla extract
- ⅔ c. sour cream
- Cinnamon-sugar mix:
    - ¼ c. sugar
    - 1 tbsp. cinnamon
- Enough peanut or vegetable oil to fill your Dutch one-third full

- Bring the oil to 340°F on 22–24 coals, or use your burner.
- Mix flour, baking powder, salt, nutmeg, and pumpkin spice together in one bowl.
- In a separate bowl, mix together well the sugar and shortening.
- Add eggs to sugar and shortening; mix well.
- Add vanilla, pumpkin, and sour cream to the egg, sugar, and shortening mixture; incorporate well
- Add wet ingredients on top of dry; and mix carefully until all the dry is wet.
- With just a touch of flour on a rolling surface, roll dough out to 1" thick.

- Cut dough into donuts with cutter or a round cup with fine edges.
- Shake excess flour off of donuts; drop carefully into hot oil.
- Cook for 15–30 seconds and then flip for 90 seconds; flip back again for 60 seconds.
- Cook until golden brown.
- Drain briefly on the rack, then sprinkle with cinnamon-sugar mix.
- Serve warm.

13 Sauces and Rubz

I'm in Dutch!

The first morn bright and large, the camp master in charge cautioned youth with a word of advice.

"You lot look atrocious, but somewhat precocious, so before acting you'd better think twice.

This week one will fall, clothes, backpack and all, in the river and get soaking wet.

Another will trip, and possibly flip, in the fire pit among the briquettes.

And still one boy more will surely ignore the advice on knife safety and sense.

So that fine young man, with knife in his hand, will slip and make a digit past tense."

The camp master stopped as the young men's eyes popped and then went blank in their gaze.

And the boys went about all the jesting, no doubt, and the advice received soon washed away.

Well, one scout went swimming after the warning was given and took with him all of his tack.

Then came the fire that seemed to conspire, and the young man fell square in its track.

And last but not least, the scout who did bleed and first aid that couldn't be finer.

Far more surprising, all the uprising, fell on one unfortunate minor.

Now you may render this story is tender when the boy informed Dad, "It was me."

Even so, more devout is when Dad told the scout, "I had to tell Gramps the same thing."

—Wade P. Haggard

Greek Sauce

- 2 tbsp. Greek seasoning:
    - 1 tbsp. oregano, dried and crushed
    - 1 tbsp. marjoram, dried and crushed
    - 2 tsp. thyme, dried and crushed
    - 1 tsp. onion powder
    - 1 tsp. garlic powder
    - 1 tsp. basil, dried and crushed
- Zest of 3 limes
- Juice of 4 limes (about ½ cup)

- Mix all ingredients thoroughly; and let sit covered in refrigerator for 8 hours.
- Use as needed.

Did you know that the French toast recipe (p. 109) can be turned into insane bread pudding? Replace the bread with 1 dozen glazed donuts, quartered. Add ½ c. sugar to your egg mixture. Follow the French toast directions!

Best BBQ Sauce Ever!

- 1 c. catsup
- ⅓ c. brown sugar
- ⅓ c. cider vinegar
- ⅓ c. Worcestershire
- 2 tbsp. The Rub (p. 181)

* Mix all ingredients in a saucepan or Dutch on 20–22 coals; bring to a boil for 2 minutes.
* Let cool, and use as needed.

Sweet 'n Sour to Die For

- 1 c. cider vinegar
- 1 c. pineapple juice
- 1 tbsp. soy sauce
- 1 tbsp. ginger, minced (fresh is best, or ½ tsp. ground)
- 1 tsp. white pepper
- 2 tbsp. cornstarch

- Mix cornstarch in pineapple juice.
- Mix all ingredients. in a saucepan or Dutch on 20–22 coals; bring to a boil for 2 minutes
- Let cool, and use as needed.

BBQ Sauce Vinegar Style

- 1 c. cider vinegar
- 1 tsp. salt
- 1 tbsp. brown sugar
- 1 tbsp. brown mustard
- ½ tsp. ground cayenne

- Mix all ingredients in a saucepan or Dutch on 20–22 coals; bring to a boil for 2 minutes.
- Let cool, and use as needed.

Tenacious Teriyaki Sauce

- 1 c. soy sauce
- ¾ c. brown sugar
- 2 tbsp. Mirin (a type of rice wine with low alcohol and high sugar content)
- 1 tsp. ground ginger
- 2 tbsp. cornstarch
- ½ c. water

- Mix all ingredients in a saucepan or Dutch on 20–22 coals; bring to a boil for 2 minutes.
- Let cool, and use as needed.

Tzatziki

- 2 c. sour cream (or use 2 c. Greek yogurt, strained)
- 1 cucumber, peeled, seeded, and shredded
- ½ tsp. salt
- 2 tbsp. lime juice
- Zest of 1 lime
- 2 tsp. garlic, minced
- Pinch of white pepper, maybe two pinches if you like pepper

- Mix all ingredients together.
- Allow to sit covered in refrigerator for 3 hours before serving.
- Enjoy on gyros, souvlaki (p. 67), or fried zucchini (p. 144).

Mexican Rub

- 1 tbsp. seasoned salt
- 4 tbsp. cumin
- 2 tsp. Mexican oregano
- 1 tbsp. chipotle powder (or chili powder)
- 1 tsp. black pepper
- 1 tsp. garlic powder
- 1 tsp. onion powder
- ¼ tsp. ground cloves

The Rub (You will need this recipe frequently.)

- o   1 tbsp. garlic powder
- o   1 tbsp. onion powder
- o   1 tsp. black pepper
- o   1 tsp. white pepper
- o   2 tbsp. smoked paprika
- o   1 tbsp. dry mustard
- o   3 tbsp. seasoned salt
- o   1 tbsp. chili powder
- o   1 tsp. ground cayenne

- Mix all the ingredients together; use as needed.
- Store in a sealed ziplock baggie.

Italian Rub

- o 1 tsp. garlic salt
- o 1 tsp. onion powder
- o 1 tsp. sugar
- o 2 tsp. dried oregano
- o ¼ tsp. pepper
- o ¼ tsp. thyme, dried
- o ¼ tsp. basil, dried
- o 1 tsp. parsley, dried
- o ¼ tsp. celery salt
- o 1 tsp. seasoned salt

- Mix all the ingredients together; use as needed.
- Store in a sealed ziplock baggie.

Vanilla Cinnamon Syrup

- 1.5 c. sugar
- ½ c. brown sugar
- 1 c. water
- 2 tbsp. vanilla extract
- 2 tsp. cinnamon
- ½ tsp. salt

- Mix all ingredients together in a saucepan, minus the butter. (You can use your Dutch on 20–22 coals for syrup, but I like a saucepan.)
- Bring to a boil for 3 minutes.
- Remove from heat; add butter, cool for 10–15 minutes.
- Serve warm.

Fruit Syrup

- 2 c. sugar
- ¾ c. water
- 1 c. favorite frozen fruit (strawberries, blueberries, mixed berries)
- 1 tsp. vanilla extract
- ½ tsp. salt

- Mix all ingredients; bring to a boil for 3 minutes, with the Dutch on 20–22 coals.
- Set aside; allow to cool for 10 minutes.
- Crush the berries.
- Serve on pancakes or waffles.

Maple Glaze

- 1 c. powdered sugar
- ¼ c. maple syrup
- ½ tsp. salt
- 2 tbsp. butter (very soft)
- 1 tsp. maple extract

* Mix all ingredients together in a small bowl.
* Add more syrup if too thick; add more sugar if too thin.
* Great on Bacon Cinnamon Rolls (p. 104).

Cream Cheese Frosting

- 1 8-oz. package cream cheese, softened
- ¼ c. butter
- 1 tsp. vanilla extract
- 1 tsp. almond extract
- 4 c. (1 16-oz. package) powdered sugar

* Mix all ingredients together until smooth.
* Serve on top of cookies, donuts, or cinnamon rolls.
* Great licked off your finger, or someone else's; I'm not picky.

Country Gravy with Sausage or Bacon

- 1 lb. ground sausage or chopped bacon (Half of each works great, too.)
- 2 tsp. black pepper
- 1 tsp. salt
- 2 12-oz. cans evaporated milk
- 4 c. milk (whole, 2 percent, or skim)
- 1 c. flour

- Heat Dutch oven on 20–22 coals.
- Brown meat; remove from Dutch and set aside.
- Remove all but about ½ c. oil from Dutch.
- Sprinkle flour over oil and mix thoroughly; cook for 3–5 minutes.
- Add all milk; whisk flour mix into milk until no lumps remain.
- Add meat, salt, and pepper.
- Bring to a gentle boil while stirring well.
- Cook for 2–3 minutes, stirring to keep from the mixture from burning or sticking to bottom of the Dutch.
- Serve on biscuits, potato pancakes (p. 103), or a slice of toast with a fried egg on top.

INDEX

Apple Pie	163
Baked Beans	150
Baked Potatoes	141
Baking Mix	89
Barbacoa De Res	46
Basic Easy Cobbler	164
BBQ Chicken	50
BBQ Pork Loin Tips	68
BBQ Sauce	177
Beef Brisket	39
Beef Pot Roast	42
Beef Ribs	40
Beer Batter	90
Berry Pie Filling	161
Biscuits	86
Bread	81
Breakfast Casserole	101
Brownies	168
Cake Style Fruit Cobbler	154
Carne Asada	38
Carnitas	73
Cheesy Biscuits	89
Cheesy Potatoes	139
Cherry Pie Filling	159
Chicken and Dumplings	59
Chicken Fajitas	62
Chicken Fingers	57
Chili and Cornbread	121
Chili with Beans	113
Chili without Beans	116
Chocolate Cake	166
Cilantro Lime Chicken	49
Cinnamon Rolls	104
Coleslaw	146
Cornbread	93
Country Gravy	185
Cream Cheese Frosting	184
Dinner Rolls	84
Dutch Fried Rice	147
Elk Roast in Bacon	136
Enchilada Casserole	119
Flat Bread	84
French Toast	109
French Fries	143
Fried Chicken	58
Fried Zucchini	144
Fruit Syrup	183
Fry Bread	88
Garlic Butter Chicken	53
German Pancake	108
Gorditas	94
Greek Sauce	176
Green Chili	69
Halibut	132
Ham and Cheese Pancakes	105
Hash Browns	142
Heavenly Pancakes	106
Hot German Potato Salad	145
Hungarian Goulash	44
Italian Beef	43
Italian Roasted Potatoes	140
Italian RUB	182
Key Lime Pie	171
Lasagna	117
Lemon Rice	149
Maple Glaze	184
Meatballs	41
Meatloaf	41
Mexican RUB	180
Oatmeal Crumble Cobbler	157
Old Fashioned Stew	125
Parker House Rolls	83
Peach Pie Filling	160
Pie Crust	90
Pineapple Upside Down Cake	169
Pizza	91
Pork and Apples	72
Pork Picnic	76
Pork Ribs	77
Pork Schnitzel	74
Pork Sirloin Tips	66
Potato Pancakes	103
Pumpkin Bread	96

Pumpkin Spice Cake	170
Pumpkin Spice Donuts	172
Quiche	99
Roast Chicken	52
Roast Pork Chop	78
Salmon	130
Sandwich Rolls	84
Sausage and Potato Stew	123
Savory Rolls	85
Shepherd's Pie	126
Shortbread Cobbler	155
Shortcake Cobbler	156
Shredded Beef Chili	115
Sourdough Biscuits	87
Sourdough Pancakes	107
Sourdough Starter	95
Souvlaki	67
Spanish Rice	148
Spice is Nice Chicken Breasts	61
Steak Pizza	92
Steak and Potatoes	35
Steak Tips	30
Steak Tips BBQ Sweet / Hot	32
Steak Tips BBQ Vinegar	33
Steak Tips Rosemary and Garlic	34
Steak Tips Teriyaki	31
Sweet N Sour Chicken	51
Sweet n Sour Pork	70
Sweet N Sour Sauce	178
Swiss Steak	36
Taco Casserole	122
Tandoori Chicken	56
Teriyaki Sauce	179
Teriyaki Chicken	55
Teriyaki Pork	71
THE RUB (BBQ)	181
Tri Tip Roast	45
Trout	131
Tzatziki	179
Vanilla Cinnamon Syrup	183
Venison or Elk Burger	135
Vinegar BBQ Sauce	178
Wild Red Meat Roast	134
Wild Red Meat Steak	133
Yellow Cake	167

ABOUT THE AUTHOR

I begin each day with an imaginative idea to pursue. Sometimes, the idea proliferates, and I enjoy the bounty of my thoughts. Some days, the idea fizzles and dies; all that remains is the comfort of an ambitious attempt and perhaps a few paragraphs of gibberish to resurrect on another day. Many activities and quite a few interactions throughout the day will find themselves tied to a story or a thought, on occasion ending as music or poetry. Often, as with the story of Esther Bunny, the simplest of questions can become an instant and an overwhelming desire to write a story from another angle or pursue an adventure in a fractured state.

I love to do things with my family, especially if it consists of camping and the ATVs. Every member of my family is considered a "food person," so I enjoy cooking; from comfort food to gourmet. The Food Network is one of my guilty pleasures. I also like to visit the gym; the exercise keeps me in balance and ready for a good hike, another of my pastimes. I draw from all these experiences to tell stories, cook, write poetry, create recipes, and compose music.

As one of my community endeavors, I volunteer as a Scoutmaster for the Boy Scouts of America as a calling in the LDS church (The Church of Jesus Christ of Latter-day Saints). The calling itself is rewarding, I enjoyed scouting as a young man, and I enjoy it now as a much older young man. Scouting is for families, and frankly, scouts are a family, in my mind. The young men I have had the opportunity to work with teach and depend on one another; they are an individual part of a greater whole. What a wonderful lesson of selflessness these youthful men learn, and at what an impressionable age. I hope to have a positive impact on their lives, as I hope, through this book, I will on yours.

Come pay me a visit, www.wadehaggard.com.

—Wade

Made in the USA
San Bernardino, CA
12 February 2016